The Penny Whistle™ Party Planner

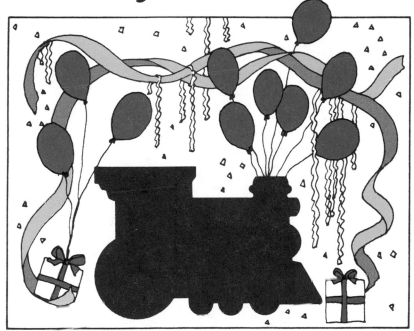

Meredith Brokaw & Annie Gilbar

DESIGNED AND ILLUSTRATED BY JILL WEBER

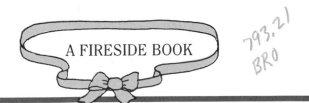

A FIRESIDE BOOK

793.21
BRO

Published by Simon & Schuster
New York   London   Toronto   Sydney   Tokyo   Singapore

FIRESIDE
Rockefeller Center
1230 Avenue of the Americas
New York, New York 10020

First Fireside Edition 1991
Published by arrangement with the authors.

Designed by Jill Weber
Manufactured in the United States of America

10 9   Pbk.

ISBN 0-671-73792-9 Pbk.

Penny Whistle Toys is a registered trademark of
Penny Whistle Toys, Inc. and is used herein by permission.

A Big Thank You to the following friends who have helped every step of the way:

Dan Green, Jill Weber, Gary Gilbar, Tom Brokaw, Angela Miller, Judith Weber, Janet Surmi, Donna Skrzypek, and Dr. Lee Salk.

And we are indebted to all the mothers and fathers, toy store owners and customers, and many special friends who shared their ideas, advice and remembrances with us:

Esther Ancoli
Pam Auld
Patrice Auld
Ruth Bloom
Sandra Brown
Ann Buchwald
Art Buchwald
Amanda Burden
Carrie Carmichael
Rosalynn Carter
Carol Chalmers
    (of The Toy Store
    in Sun Valley, Idaho)
Madeline Chandler
Janet Coberly
Nora Ephron
Donnie Epp
Marie Evans
Vilma Farman
Dorrit Ger
    (of the Pied Piper in
    Manhasset, New York)
Andrea Garr
Mary Ellen Geisser
Beth Gibbons
Sylvia Gilbar
Julian Goodman
Bobbie Gordon
Robby Gordon
Ronna Gordon
David Halberstam
Jean Halberstam

Millie Harmon
Inadoll Harvey
Marcia Herman
Ann Hollister
Margo Howard
Sonia Ancoli Israel
Beau James
Suzanne Jeffers
Gerri Karetsky
Charlotte Kriegel
Jay Kriegel
Carole Lalli
Leslie Auld Larson
Jessica Leader
Jo Lewis
Heather McCorkindale
Laura McCorkindale
Lisa Meers
Marilyn Melton
Polly Merrill
Myra Miller
Stuart Miller
Margaret Montgomery
Gloria Nagy
Teresa Nathanson
Maureen Orth
Jan Platt
Maryann Pope
Bobbi Queen
Pam Rafanowicz
Ira Reiner
Jane Reynolds

Jennifer Ridgeway
Rick Ridgeway
Hilly Ripmaster
Lynda Johnson Robb
Nancy Rubin
Susan Russell
Tim Russert
Carol Schneider
Nan Schwartz
Nancy Seastrom
Mary Slawson
Jean Kennedy Smith
Lynne Sprecher
Susan Strauss
Geraldine Stutz
Betty Takeuchi
    (of the San Marino
    Toy & Bookshoppe)
Janice Treadwell
Alice Trillin
Calvin Trillin
Maggie Moss Tucker
Suzanne Turman
Louise Vaughan
Laurie Waldstein
Diane Wayne
Delores Wharton
Stacey Winkler
Phyllis Wolff
Ellen Wright
Richard Wurman
Jessica Yellin

CONTENTS

For Jennifer, Andrea,
        Sarah, Lisa and Marc

Who together have planned,
given and enjoyed, at last count,
63 unforgettable birthday parties

INTRODUCTION

O ne of the wonderful things about having children is that you can relive childhood again. It's not the lost dreams or the chance to do a report on the differences between Neanderthal and Cro-Magnon man or twenty problems in long division. Rather, it is having the chance to share laughter, wonder, joy and fun with your child. Children have a way of seeing things simply, of putting things in a natural perspective and knowing their priorities. Celebrations are high on the list. Mention Christmas and children's eyes suddenly glow. Just allude to a birthday party and the world stops around them.

Children believe that their birthday, the date circled in red on the calendar, marks all other events. ("School starts after my birthday." "Spring is before my birthday." "Independence Day is just before my birthday.") It's the celebration of their personal new year. Most importantly, a child's birthday is an opportunity for parents to share this special time together with their child. It is an opportunity not to be missed.

Your child's party could, and should, be fun for everyone. Kids just want to have fun, and so do their parents. Parties are occasions for everyone to enjoy, but why does the mere mention of planning a birthday party make some parents start to hyperventilate? How can the process of arranging, organizing and preparing for a birthday party bring even the strongest, sanest, most successful of parents to tears? Why do we know parents who would rather arrange a sit-down dinner for fifty than a two-hour birthday party for ten five-year-olds?

If you don't have the tools at hand, if you let anxiety instead of joy rule, planning a party for your child can be hectic, frustrating, annoying, difficult and overwhelming.

We come across this problem every day. One of our favorite customers at the Penny Whistle Toy Stores, a woman who runs her own business and who has always seemed like such a take-charge person, appeared at the store one day almost totally unnerved as she related this story:

" 'Mom,' said my five-year-old son. 'What are we going to do for my birthday party this year?'

"I felt that familiar panic enveloping me and thought to myself, What are the chances that he would forget about having a party this year and instead let us fly him to Disney World? None! He has been marking off the days on his calendar since the last birthday party. I thought maybe we could bribe him with an incredible gift instead of inviting his entire class to our house, but the fact is that there wasn't a chance I could talk him out of a party, and I knew it.

"But how do I explain to a five-year-old what it has taken for me to plan, prepare for and execute a birthday party? Would he understand that the stress that tightened my chest and made my head pound was due, pure and simple, to total panic at the thought of undertaking yet another children's party? Would he wonder why his mother, who takes care of business, who entertains adults at the drop of a hat, is still terrified of tackling a bunch of children for a couple of hours one day a year?"

She's not alone. Another family we know decided to have a three-hour Superman party for their three-year-old son. Things did not go quite as they had hoped. Superman arrived an hour late, his cape forgotten on his kitchen counter, his red eyes bloodshot from the stress of having just finished another party for twenty three-year-olds. This "Superflake" finished his rather lame act in ten minutes and the family was then faced with yet another hour to entertain fifteen restless, tired, disappointed and bored kids. They served lunch, but the food was not attractive and the kids were uninterested in it. As a last resort, they gave out the party favors earlier than planned and then sat around and watched the clock, convinced that during a birthday party there are at least one hundred minutes in every hour.

Then there was the time a mother planned a spring backyard picnic for her four-year-old daughter's birthday. She sent out plastic shovels as invitations, with the information printed on a label pasted on the back of each shovel. Those were a huge hit and the plans sounded great. They poured extra sand in the backyard, stocked up on hot dogs and hamburgers for the barbecue, and invited Mr. Picklepockets to entertain.

But the day came and no one was prepared for the unexpected. The party was called for noon. It started raining—no, pouring—at 12:02. The sand turned into mud. The food, which was so efficiently and neatly arranged on a platter near the barbecue so it would be ready to go, was soaked. There was no contingency plan to handle the unpredictable April weather. The outside games didn't work in the living room. And Mr. Picklepockets was so crotchety and short-tempered that they admitted considering drowning him in the little lake that was once their backyard.

We could swap children's party stories forever. Most are funny; some are head-shakers; others make us shudder at the memories. But there is something to be learned from these stories, which is that parents need the right tools to give a successful children's party; that such a party needs to be carefully planned, totally orchestrated, imaginatively created, and then given with humor, confidence and love.

We are here to put your party-giving anxieties to rest, so that the parties you give from now on are joyous experiences from beginning to end.

Parties can—and should—be wonderful! If we plan ahead and prepare for those unexpected catastrophes, if we have parties that are original and appropriate for that age group so the activities don't get out of hand or the lack of them doesn't leave us all high and dry, if everyone is involved in the planning so there are as few surprises as possible, and if we try to keep the cost down, then celebrating with your child becomes a joy.

Both the planning and the execution of your child's party should be fun for you and your child. And it is this fun (and not the number of dancing elephants you have hired), this energy and love, your positive and happy attitude, which will result in a closeness and sharing of a wonderful experience that will make it a memorable event for everyone.

After all, children *are* fun, games *are* fun, and entertaining *is* fun. Why can't a party be fun, too?

At Penny Whistle we have gathered lots of knowledge and experience. By talking to mothers, fathers, teachers, professional party givers, entertainers, child psychologists and Penny Whistle customers, we found that there *are* ways to make children's parties wonderful occasions. There are ways to plan appropriate activities that are as infallible as possible, to create unique, wondrous fantasy environments, to prepare easy and inexpensive menus—in short, to have a party for your child that is both special for him and a pleasure for both of you.

The ideas, plans, tools and support are all here. These will help you get the confidence you will need to successfully plan and execute your child's party. By the time you are ready to choose a party with your child, you will have at your fingertips everything you need to know about giving children's parties. We'll take you, step by step, through more than thirty parties, from designing the invitation to collecting the decorations to planning the games and menu and choosing the favors. You'll find out how to choose a theme, how to coordinate and make the invitations, how to buy and/or make the food and give out the most unusual and exciting party favors that will be the talk of kid-town.

If we suggest using ballet tutus for party favors then we will show you how to make them or where to buy them. You want to bake a cake in the shape of a bear? We'll show you how to do that, too—and where to buy teddy bears for decorations and how to make a teddy bear cutout. Want to have a Space party and need some special effects? It's all here. You'll find variations on the same old classic games, as well as many other games to occupy young kids, plus more adventurous and challenging games for older children. Does your child have her heart set on a Ghost party? Don't panic—it's easy to make goblin invitations and "Slime Jell-O," and to turn your kid's room into a ghost haven so that they'll giggle with delight at the movie-like effects.

And there's much more—hints on photographing and recording a party; on choosing a place, entertainer and theme; on involving other parents, family and friends; on dealing with unexpected problems and last-minute decision-making; and on keeping the cost at what you can afford. You'll find drawings you can reproduce, recipes you can make and, on each page, special hints to make your party successful and special.

The Penny Whistle Party Planner is just the kind of book we wish we had years ago and are glad we can share with you now.

GIVING A PARTY
AND LOVING IT

THE PENNY WHISTLE PRINCIPLES OF PARTY PLANNING

1. It's Worth It!

Our most important and basic belief is that it's worth the trouble to plan a home birthday party for your child. This doesn't mean spending a lot of money or planning a lavishly overindulgent party, but rather spending your energy and time planning something your child will love and always remember.

Sarah Brokaw still tells stories of her Safari party twelve years after it happened. Thirty-five years later, Jay Kriegel still remembers the Backwards party his mom gave. Eight years later, Lisa Gilbar remembers her Raggedy Ann and Andy party, with a Scavenger Hunt for eggs that netted baskets full of jelly beans in all sizes and colors. And though her sons are now teenagers, Nancy Rubin still brings out the same crown and birthday banner on their birthdays. And the authors themselves (more years later than we are going to tell you) can still recount who came to their parties, what they wore, who won that treasure hunt and who got to sleep the latest at their slumber parties.

2. Do It Yourself

We don't mean do it alone, Supermom and Superdad. But we do mean, don't take the easier (and more impersonal) way out by hiring a party planner and, on the day of the party, opening the door, letting him in and making out a check. This is your child's party, and it should be as uniquely and personally hers as you can make it. Anyone can hire a party planner to "do" a party. There's nothing personal about it—and there will be another two dozen just like it. Moreover, employing someone to orchestrate a party that any other child can (and will) have undercuts the entire point of giving a party for your child: It is a personal occasion, and making it so is up to you and your child.

Child psychologist (and parent) Dr. Lee Salk explains it this way: "There is an attitude nowadays in our society that other people can do things better for your children. That's just not true. There is nothing personally creative about hiring someone else to put together your party. And the messages you give your child are: I can't be bothered with doing it myself. I don't have the time to do this for you. I can't wait for this to be over. I don't want to mess up my house. I don't want to be involved so I'll give you this prepackaged (and often expensive) party."

By delegating this wonderful responsibility to an outsider you will find that you are missing a great opportunity for your family to share this experience together. To make it easier we have done much of the work. Now all you have to do is make choices, follow the guidelines and suggestions, and select a flexible party program that is just what you and your child want. We want you to make this party *yours*.

3. Plan the Party with Your Child

Whether this is a birthday party or a holiday party, it is your child's party. These words may seem obvious to you, but give them some thought. Understanding that this is your child's party, and not your own, is crucial to the success of the party. It is his moment so he should share in all aspects of the planning and decision-making involved in the birthday party. Obviously, we are not speaking of children who are only a year old, but even your two-year-old can tell you that he adores Mickey Mouse or that she just has to have Peter Pan at her party. Participation and involvement in every part of the decision-making process is very important to making your child feel involved in the process of planning his party. It will also do wonders for his self-esteem!

Again, Dr. Lee Salk: "Your child's birthday is such an important social event in his or her life. It is a great opportunity for the family to come together and discuss things, for a child to participate actively in the decision-making process. It is important for every human being to have some impact on his own environment (for example, if a child is constantly told what to do and taught to be blindly obedient, it takes away his sense of self and can make him feel helpless). Kids need choices, and this is a great time to give them the chance to make them."

This does not mean that your child must have the final word on all the decisions, but if you consult him you'll be surprised how much more all of you will enjoy the planning process.

Consider what your child loves: What are his current passions? Who is her favorite hero? What games does he love to play? What kind of party does she want to have? The fact that you even asked your child these questions will make him feel important, and the answers will help to narrow down the choices you have to make.

Listen to these answers. Even if they may present added problems or greater difficulties (you found a terrific puppeteer, but Jeremy wants to have a Scavenger Hunt; Pam dreams of having an Olympics party with the entire class, while you had hoped to get by with a Pizza party for six), try to compromise and fulfill your child's party dreams. And don't try to talk your child into having a party you would like. Chances are pretty good it will backfire! Several years ago Annie's son Marc dreamed of having a Ghost party. Annie and her husband had planned a Magic party and convinced Marc that it would be terrific. It was a good party, and Marc and his friends had a fine time, but several weeks later, Marc mentioned quietly, "Magic was fun, but I really wish I'd had a Ghost party."

Sharing the party planning process with your child will make her feel as if she is the most special child in the world—and it will make it fun for all of the family. And that means sharing a lot of things. If you can arrange it, take your child with you to choose the invitations, decorations and favors. When you contemplate the menu, talk over the choices with your child. Choose the games together as well. And later, when it comes time to prepare for the party, you can make things together. You'll be surprised at how much fun your child will have coloring the invitations, putting stickers on the envelopes, giving the final okay on the menu choices and gathering the items for the decorations.

And, you'll see, this process of making choices together will give you an opportunity to listen to your child express his opinions and will show him that you respect his judgments. The power that you give your child at this time can be an important cornerstone in your relationship with him; it will relieve some of the stress that your child is bound to feel about the upcoming activities; and, most of all, you and your child will have fun planning this special day.

4. Temper Your Expectations

It's so easy to get carried away planning a party! It is important to keep the process and the event in perspective. This is, after all, only a party, not an international summit meeting. It is supposed to be fun. The better prepared you are, the better your party will be. If the unexpected happens, you will handle it. If a game is a bust, it's not a tragedy. Remember, children just want to have a good time and don't need total perfection to be happy.

5. Both Parents Should Be at the Party

Carol Chalmers of The Toy Store in Sun Valley, Idaho, has been performing as a clown at local birthday parties for about eight years. Says Carol, "Parties with both parents present always work better." On this special day it is important for both parents to be there, if at all possible.

6. Parties are Theater—Plan for Every Moment

A party is theater. Planning it is just like constructing a play. You have a beginning, a middle and an end, and every minute is accounted for. Having such a complete plan, a feeling of great control, will virtually guarantee that your party will be a success.

The First Act—The Beginning • It is a given that children do not arrive at a party all at one time. Therefore you will need to be able to keep the children busy as they arrive. You will find that many of our parties have a game that can be played by those prompt arrivals. Other parties have tasks designed for these first kids so they will feel welcome and at ease.

Act Two—The Middle • This is the body of the party, where the activities take place. We have included suggested games and activities in each party to fill at least two hours (depending on the party and the ages of the children). Planning more games than you think you'll need gives you the flexibility to move on from a game that the children don't like, or add a game if they finish one sooner than you had planned. By building in these contingencies, you will never find yourself with children everywhere and nothing to keep them occupied.

Act Three • At this time, after playing several games, the children will need a quieter time. This is a good time to move directly into serving the food. They will be seated, will devour the food, sing their birthday songs and slowly begin to unwind from the more hectic activities. At some of our parties we have suggested several quiet table games the children can play.

Act Four—The Denouement • After they have eaten, you can gather the children around and involve them in the final activities. If you have made a videotape of the party, you can show it at this time. Then you can help your child distribute the party favors. By this time the parents should be arriving to collect their children. If some children are still waiting for their parents, gather this small group and let them help you with clean-up activities and putting the gifts away.

And this brings us to gifts.

7. Opening Gifts

We have our own opinions on the ritual of gift giving, but deciding whether or not to have your child open his gifts at the birthday party is up to you.

Children like to open gifts in front of their friends, and their guests take pleasure in seeing the birthday child's reaction to the gift each of them has brought. After all, half the fun of giving a gift is seeing the recipient enjoy it! A good time to do this is after the food has been served and eaten.

Even the politest of children can forget a "thank you" in the rush and excitement of a birthday party. Thus it might be appropriate to spend some time before the party going over some obvious yet important thoughts about gifts. Try to stress that the thought does count—expensive does not mean best. It's a good opportunity to teach your child to be as thoughtful and kind about a small gift as a large one. (This is difficult for a lot of kids because "big" is usually synonymous with "impressive." But it is an important point because a child who has brought a small gift is just as proud of her gift.)

You might discuss the problem of the duplicate present. The gift a guest has brought is important to him, and he will be anxious to see a reaction. If your child already has the gift, a kind thing to say might be, "Thanks so much! I love this toy so much that I already have it!" If it is something she really doesn't like, suggest that she can be polite by saying something simple like, "Thank you for your thoughtfulness" or "Thank you for this gift."

Then there is the matter of thank you notes. If your child cannot write, make sure he thanks the guest at the time of the party—and that's it. If your child can write, the thank you note is a very nice way of letting his guests know that he really appreciated the gift.

8. Take an Active Part

One aspect of taking an active part—being totally involved in the planning of your child's party—is something we have already advocated. But an added thought is being involved in the actual party process. This means not only being there at all times but participating in the activities. Play the games or at least be the referee or organizer with your child. If the children are on the floor, get down there with them. If they are in a race or participating in the Scavenger Hunt, go along. You've already cooked the food, set the table—now share in the fun!

Our friend Susan Strauss is a wonderful example of a mother who truly participates in her son Jonathan's parties. Not only does she plan the details and the themes with him, but on the day of the party, she is there, joining the children in the fun. Many of her friends have been surprised when Susan, who normally dresses very fashionably, greets them and their children at the door in full costume. When Jonathan had a Peter Pan party, he was Peter Pan and she was the Indian Princess, complete with brown tights, a leather skirt and a feathered hat. And when it was Superman's turn, she was Supergirl, with red and blue tights, a handmade satin cape and headband.

And when anyone asks Jonathan about his birthday parties, he always mentions that his mom "always dresses up just like me!" With such personal gestures to her son, Susan has made his parties memorable and made Jonathan very proud.

STAGE ONE — six weeks ahead
STAGE TWO — four weeks ahead
STAGE THREE — two weeks ahead
STAGE FOUR — the day before

9. Plan Ahead

Give yourself plenty of time to plan a party. There is enough to do within a six-week period at a comfortable, leisurely pace, giving you lots of time to accomplish everything. If you don't leave yourself enough time, you are adding stress that you don't need. All you have to do is follow the guidelines, feeling free to add to or subtract from them. Giving yourself extra time makes it more fun and much easier!

Our parties are divided into stages. Ideally, Stage One begins six weeks ahead, Stage Two four weeks ahead, Stage Three two weeks ahead and Stage Four the day before the party. As is our philosophy, this schedule is flexible. If you find that you must begin to plan your party two weeks ahead, just do it—and combine and condense the stages.

You'll also find that some parties have four stages and some five because some parties need less lead time for preparation and others include things that need to be done that very morning.

Two lessons, then: Give yourself as much time as possible to plan the party. And if you can't, don't panic! Follow our guidelines and everything will fall into place.

10. Making Guest Lists

Guest lists for pre-schoolers will be your own. After the age of three or four, your child needs to be consulted.

First, how many children do you invite? A rule of thumb that some people use is to invite as many children as the child's age (a five-year-old, for example, would invite five children). The benefit of having small groups is that it's easier to handle the guests and give each child the attention she needs.

If your child's teacher has asked that no children be left out of a party, this means that the entire class must be invited. Don't panic! Most of our parties can easily accommodate twenty kids or so. Besides, this is actually a very sensitive way to deal with children's feelings; being left out of a party can be a trauma for a child (and many an adult!). Thus inviting everyone in a class (or all the girls or boys) is a thoughtful way to go. This happened one year to Meredith's daughter Sarah, who was adamant that a girl who had not been invited to other parties come to her party since Sarah wanted to be sure her feelings would not be hurt. Several years later, the child's mother met Meredith and told her how much it had meant to her daughter to be included.

Our parties are geared to handle a few or many children; you can easily increase or decrease the number of guests (with the exception of the Chefs in the Kitchen party, where too many chefs could spoil the broth and for which the size of the guest list should be determined by the size of your kitchen).

Some parties lend themselves to inviting neighbors, relatives and friends outside school. If you would rather limit the number of children at the birthday party, you could have a separate family dinner to celebrate the birthday.

Another question that will inevitably come up is whether to invite both girls and boys. At certain ages, boys and girls like to go to parties together, usually before age five and after age twelve. In between, they often profess to not being able to stand each other. The choice of inviting girls or boys is up to you and your child—these parties can work for both.

11. Get Help

You do not have to give a party alone. Get help! Ask your neighbors, relatives or friends to help the day of the party. Hire some high school students to help organize or to entertain the children (see our suggestions for using high school kids under each party). You will need help, so ask for it!

12. That Personal Touch Is Important

You'll find that in our parties we make a lot of things because the personal touch is simply more meaningful. In each party we have combined items that you can buy with those that you and your child can make. Take the time to try these; they are simple, and it will mean a lot to everyone that you took the trouble. Use our ideas or let them trigger your own.

13. Forget Competition!

The idea is not to outdo anybody, but rather to personalize your own party. Extravaganzas are unnecessary and sometimes stand out in a negative way. Don't overdo; spending a lot of money may send the wrong message to your child. This is a child's party, so don't give it the feeling of a lavish adult party. Forget the fireworks—make a birthday banner and your child will remember it forever.

14. Dealing with Siblings

This is the birthday child's day. But that does not mean that his sister or brother must be ignored. Parent after parent we talked with told us that they always included the siblings. (If a sibling does not want to be there, it's easy to have him spend that time at a friend's house. But it seems that in more cases than not, siblings hate to miss out on any action going on at home.) Have the sister invite her special friend over for that day. They can either play apart from the party or be helpers.

You can also have the birthday child assign special duties to his brother. He could be in charge of a game, greet guests or collect presents. If you give the sibling something specific to do, he will not feel left out and can actually be helpful at the party.

15. Age-Appropriate Parties

You are the best judge of what is appropriate for your child's age, but you need to make such a conscious decision. To help you decide, we have geared our parties towards children of specific ages. Some are designed for children from the age of four to about eight; others are better given for children eight to twelve. And Chapter Two is totally devoted to parties appropriate to children ages one to three. Since you know your child best, you should decide whether a particular theme is right or not. *The Penny Whistle Party Planner* will guide you about age range with each event.

Don't assume that eleven- or twelve-year-olds don't like games. They may try to act older and more sophisticated but they love games! Playing games also takes the pressure off trying to be cool and so grown-up. They'll participate with glee!

You might want to keep this thought in mind: Children have a lot of time in which they can become adults; they don't need to be urged to grow up any faster. If other mothers are urging girls to have boys at their parties or giving make-up parties for eight-year-olds, and this seems inappropriate for your child (and your child is uncomfortable with such plans), buck the trend and stick to your guns. Knowing your own values and the personality of your child will guide you in making appropriate decisions that will make you and your child happy.

16. Be Flexible

One of the things we like most about our parties is that they afford as much flexibility as you want. We have designed and organized complete parties with over 150 games, but many of their parts are interchangeable. If your child loves the Space party but also can't wait to play one of the games included in the Olympics party, just add it to your Space party. The same is true for our suggestions for favors and menus. These ideas and recommendations are just those—they are not mandatory. Our parties can be interchanged or left as they are. It is also our hope that the ideas you read about here will trigger your own creativity. We encourage you to either improvise on our ideas with your child or just plan your parties letting our outlines assist you.

17. Keep the Cost Down

As we've said, the parties in this book are flexible, so you can use all or some of our suggestions. We have also given a great deal of thought to the cost of the games, activities, decorations and favors. That's why you will find that we list a choice of items you can buy or make according to your time and your budget.

A great party is not necessarily an expensive one. Some parents spend a large (and perhaps inappropriate) amount of money on their children's parties and the result is not a better, prettier or happier party, but often one that embarrasses the guests with unseemly riches and extravagant gestures.

This is a party for your child and his friends. It need not impress other parents; it is not supposed to make headlines or set any records. It is a personal tribute to your child that should be as appropriate in its values and scope as in its chosen games and foods. Ten times out of ten your child will remember the care you put into the planning, the love you gave in the commitment of time and energy, the warmth and smiles you showed at the party, rather than the amount of money you spent on showy extras.

18. Take Pictures!

Both you and your child will want to remember the party. Take lots of pictures! Assign this task to some of your helpers; you have enough to do. And do it at the beginning of the party. You don't want to suddenly remember to photograph the party only to find it half over. Use your video camera if you have one (you can also rent one), and play the tape back at the end of the party—the children will love seeing themselves! Polaroid photographs of each child make wonderful party favors. If you are using 35mm. film, you may want to duplicate special photographs of the guests and send them to the parents after the party.

PLANNING THE PARTY

For each party, listed in Chapter Three, you will find instructions, suggestions and ideas for creating invitations, selecting and preparing for the activities, setting and preparing the menu, buying the decorations and favors, and selecting and hiring the entertainment. We have included a suggested (and adaptable) time frame for planning the party, an outline of things you need to make and buy, and an actual schedule of activities.

Before you turn directly to the actual parties, here is more general information on preparing for your child's party which we feel is crucial and which will make this book easier to use.

1. The Invitations

It is just as easy to use creative, imaginative and unusual materials in extraordinary ways and to send them (or have them delivered in your neighborhood) in unforgettable packages as it is to buy them at the store. Designing and planning the invitation is an important beginning to planning the party. It sets the stage and gets the guests excited long before the party happens. When they receive wooden mixing spoons or fortune cookies or balloons to blow up, the anticipation begins as the mood for an exciting party is set.

Each party in this book has its own suggested invitation (sometimes more than one), and each gives you everything you will need to create it. We provide actual drawings that you can xerox and use as ready-made invitations. And to these you can always add your own personal touch. Choose your own object to send, have your child color our drawings in, or add sequins or feathers or any accessories your child adores.

Stickers are the perfect answer to many decorating needs. They spruce up thematic invitations, are perfect for making envelopes eye-catching and will turn ordinary paper into pretty wrapping paper. Use them often to carry out your theme.

2. Length of Party

Decide on the length of time of your party. A long party isn't necessarily a successful one. As a matter of fact, a two-hour party that is well planned and chock-full of activities is a guaranteed success, whereas a disorganized gathering for four hours is a sure disaster.

3. Organizing Help

Gather your help and let them know the schedule of the party. Acquaint them with the children, the games and the food. Here's a good rule of thumb: You need one adult for every five young children (up to five years old) and one for every eight older kids.

4. Decorations

Atmosphere in a party is everything. The most ordinary of parties will be extra special if the surroundings are whimsical, surprising, and in keeping with the overall theme. Once you and your child have chosen the theme, you will find ideas for how to use wonderful objects (often the most ordinary gadgets or toys) to turn your house into your child's fantasy.

Our suggestions should inspire your own ideas. You will also find that we suggest just enough decoration to create a festive atmosphere rather than produce an overwhelming extravaganza. We urge you not to overdo it. You can design the "space" environment for the Space party without borrowing the *Apollo* space capsule from NASA. You can create a water heaven in your backyard without owning an Olympic swimming pool. You most certainly can have a Ballet party without renting the backdrop for *The Nutcracker*. Remember, more, bigger, or more expensive is not necessarily better. In fact, being extravagant with your decor may overpower your child and take the attention away from him. Our guidelines are for a simple yet effective and imaginative fantasy that should transport your guests into a party wonderland.

5. Activities

Each of our parties comes with its own set of suggested activities and games that we have designed to coincide with the theme of that party. This doesn't mean that you can't use a game from one party in another party with a different theme. Choose whatever games you and your child want to include in your party.

You will find that there are more games suggested for each party than you are likely to need. That is because we think it is better to be prepared with extra activities than to be caught with extra time on your hands. Don't be overwhelmed with the number of games we include for each party; they are there for your picking.

We indicate for each game the appropriate age of the children; the number of players needed; and which games are loud, require a lot of running around, and should be followed by games that are calming. (If you play three relays in a row and don't follow them with a silent writing game, you may find yourself surrounded by an uncontrollable mob.) We have deliberately combined both kinds of games at each party. When making up your own list of games, particularly if you are mixing and matching games from different parties, be sure to keep in mind that rowdy games need to be followed by quiet ones.

6. Entertainment

If you follow our general advice and plan to have your party last for no more than two, possibly three hours, you will find that time will be amply filled. If, however, you have decided to have a party that lasts longer, you may find that some sort of entertainment is necessary. Or you may simply choose to substitute a form of entertainment for a couple of our games.

There is a simple rule about choosing entertainment: Check it out before you hire. If you want to hire a clown, magician, storyteller or puppeteer, go see the performer at another party first. You can simply ask for references and check them out, but if it is at all possible, try to see for yourself. Meredith once hired an animal trainer for a party for Sarah. He turned out to be able to handle the children, but his choice of animals was unfortunate (you can read the whole story in the Safari party, page 178). Annie hired a magician whom a friend had used. He turned out to be a real sourpuss—he embarrassed the then three-year-old Marc, who ended up in tears, his jokes were geared towards twenty-year-olds, and his magic was mediocre. Apparently, what was okay for Annie's friend did not fit Annie's own level of expectation.

So the rule is, to minimize disappointments, check out any entertainment yourself.

You will find that we have suggested hiring high school students or other amateurs or local talent for entertainment. We have found from our experience, and from talking to mothers all over the country, that these so-called amateurs are often quite successful as entertainers. First of all, they have not performed at countless parties, so their acts will not be as predictable nor as tired. Second, the freshness and eagerness of such amateurs will more than compensate for their relative lack of sophistication or experience. Amateur high school magicians are a delight for children; their enthusiasm and ability to relate to children is matchless.

7. Food

What's a party without food? Not a party, that's what! Every child knows that, and for children, food is often a star attraction. "When are we having the cake?" Ever hear that before?

Planning is the key, and we have done that for you. We have formulated complete menus for every party. Each has been thought out both for its theme and its nutrition, and that's not so easy! It would be a great world if we could bake all the cakes without any sugar and serve only carrot sticks, granola and bean sprouts for birthday party food. Unfortunately, it doesn't seem realistic. Consequently, our suggestions include recipes with some ingredients that you may ordinarily limit. You must use your own judgment, keeping in mind that sugar is delicious but not particularly good for children, that chocolate is yummy but messy, and that ice cream is all of the above. It may, however, be a day for special dispensations!

We aimed to relate our menus directly to the theme of the party. But you will also find that you can switch the dishes. If you just love that Crater Cake (page 236) but are not giving a Space party, so what! Make it and decorate it to fit your party. Furthermore, the dishes are easy to make either the day before or that morning. You'll find that the menus are simple, easy to prepare and pretty to boot.

An added note: If you find yourself overloaded with things to do, remember that you always have the option to order a pizza!

8. Party Favors

Children don't consider the cost, but they do feel that taking something special home with them is crucial to the success of the party. And they're no fools! You can be sure that a party favor that has already been given out at all the other parties or one that falls apart before your guest gets home will be discussed and disparaged at a powwow in the schoolyard the next day.

We strongly advocate not spending a lot of money on favors. It is the unusual party favor, the one that relates to the theme of the party, that is the memorable one, especially if the kids have made it themselves. At the end of each party, you will find a list of suggested favors that were chosen with the theme of the party in mind, the cost kept at a minimum (although we have given you a choice), and the appropriate age of the children in mind.

You will also find that we suggest you choose the favors at least a couple of weeks ahead of time in the party schedule so you have time to order, make or buy the ones you really want instead of settling for last-minute replacements.

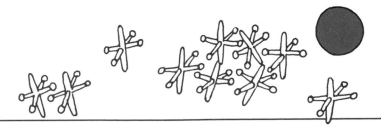

9. The Unexpected

In every party something unexpected happens. And there is not too much you can do about it, unless you know the number of a reliable fortune-teller. What you can do is the following:

A. Have a lot of help around the house so each child will have the proper amount of supervision. That will usually take care of a tearful moment or an unruly child.

B. Be prepared to deal with a child who refuses to listen. The best rule we can think of is to immediately separate this child from the others and deal with his discomfort or anger right away but elsewhere. If you can calm such a child as you would your own, with a lot of patience and some adult guile (bribery works—don't pooh-pooh offering an unhappy child an extra candy or a special job to do), such a problem will be resolved easily.

Explains Dr. Lee Salk: "This is not the time to have a public confrontation with a young guest (nor do you want to embarrass him). But it is also unacceptable to let such a child disrupt your child's party. The best method of dealing with a child who refuses to listen is to take him aside to another room and make it clear that you have rules of behavior in your home and you expect everyone to respect them." Dr. Salk suggests dealing with the child in the following manner: Say, "I'm glad you are here to be part of the party but we have certain rules here and you have to obey them." And, he adds, "You may be surprised at how effective the simple words 'Stop it!' are."

There is yet another kind of child—an observer. Such a child is often uncomfortable participating in a lot of games and is content to watch. Again, Dr. Salk: "Not everyone has to participate—some children prefer to be on the sidelines. It's best not to make this child uncomfortable, nor to pressure him to join the group (and this is definitely not the time to try any therapy!). Make sure the child knows you are happy to see him, and let him join the activities at his own pace."

C. Be sure that you have some rudimentary first aid available (Band-Aids, ice cubes, etc.).

D. If your weatherman was wrong again, and the weather has turned on you, know that all our parties can be held outdoors or indoors (except for the Backyard Beach party and the Olympics party, which can only take place outdoors and which you should plan only in the summer months when the chance of rain is minimal).

E. Each menu calls for a certain amount of extra food, so you should never run out of anything! It is easy to have extra sandwiches, pizza, cookies or drinks.

F. The chance of running out of games is also minimal, since we have provided you with extra games for every party. You'll be far more relaxed if you have planned for extra games. If you find that one game is not popular, you will be able to stop it immediately and start another. If you somehow play all the games you planned for and still have more time, having that extra game or two at your fingertips will prevent restless children from becoming unhappy and causing a disturbance.

G. Have extras of almost everything—food, favors, balloons, prizes, etc. You don't want to be caught in a bind if an extra child arrives (some parents may bring a guest's sibling without telling you) or if something breaks. Be sure to have a favor and balloon for your child. Sometimes we forget that the birthday child also gets a favor, even though she stays home after the party.

Now for the parties!

2

THE FIRST PARTIES:
THREE
AND
TWO
ONE,

THE FIRST PARTY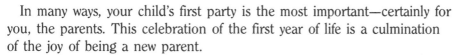

In many ways, your child's first party is the most important—certainly for you, the parents. This celebration of the first year of life is a culmination of the joy of being a new parent.

That's fine, as long as you realize that this first party is really for you and your friends. A one-year-old child is too young to understand what a birthday is or to appreciate the birthday party. As far as your child is concerned, if you gave him a cupcake with a candle on it and sang him "Happy Birthday" it would make just as much of an impact as catering a bash for twenty.

This does not mean that you should not celebrate your child's first birthday. For some of us it is important to publicly share the joy of a child's first birthday. And if you take lots of pictures, you will be able to show them to your child when he is old enough to appreciate the plans you made just for him.

Our friends Tim Russert and Maureen Orth were overjoyed at the birth of their long-awaited son Luke, and when it came time for his first birthday, they planned a unique celebration that included their whole family. They arranged a "Birthday Tour" (much like a rock 'n' roll tour) to commemorate Luke's birthday. They had T-shirts made for themselves and the grandparents that said, "Baby Luke's Birthday Tour" (with a picture of a baby in a playpen holding up a bear instead of a torch). The back of the shirt said, "1986—Buffalo, August 23; New York, August 24, and San Francisco, August 25" (the stops on the "tour").

The celebration began in Buffalo, where they visited one set of grandparents. It then continued to the big party at the Russert-Orth home in New York. There the guest list included forty friends, plus eleven babies. There were balloons everywhere, a buffet for the adults and a playpen for the baby guests with a sign that read "VIP Guests." Everyone had a grand time, and the jubilee was recorded on video to show Luke when he grows older. The "tour" continued to San Francisco so the other set of grandparents could share in the family joy.

It truly was a memorable party for the family. Explains Tim, "The party was a celebration for us, the parents. We know Luke won't remember the festivities himself. But we will show him the pictures when he's older so he can see how much we all loved him. The party was very special to us. It was a reaffirmation of his birth, a day we treasure."

SECOND AND THIRD BIRTHDAYS

By your child's second birthday she is a toddler who enjoys celebrations and relishes being the center of attention. By this age she is able to relate to other children and will be eager to enjoy a birthday bash. Chances are, too, that she has some explicit dislikes and loves, and is not shy about expressing them.

This is the time to begin planning what will really be your child's first party—at least, the first party she can help you plan and will fully participate in.

Choose the Theme with Your Child

It is your child's party, so listen to his ideas and let him choose the theme. It is not too early to encourage your child's participation in the planning of his own party. This does not mean that your two-year-old should run the show (as well he might try!), but it is important to listen when he voices his special likes. And whatever it is, planning a party around his favorite theme will be simple and fun. Here are some ideas for first parties from our friends.

Mickey Mouse • It was no secret that Courtney Jeffers adored Mickey Mouse, so when Courtney was two years old her mom, Suzanne, planned a Mickey Mouse party. Suzanne and Courtney decorated the house with every Mickey Mouse animal and doll that Courtney had collected. Mom bought other inexpensive Mickey Mouse accessories and placed them all around the party room and table. With an MM cookie cutter, peanut butter sandwiches became little Mickey Mouses. A favorite Disney record provided the most appropriate and favorite music. And Mickey Mouse ears were popular favors!

Colors • Sarah Israel adores rainbows, so when she was three Sarah and her parents arranged a small party full of rainbow surprises. It was Sarah's idea to ask the guests to come dressed as their favorite color in the rainbow. It was her idea to cover her play table with a tablecloth with rainbow designs, to stack her oversized crayons in the middle and to hang her padded rainbow over the center (this is one industrious three-year-old!). But it was Mom's idea to attach a rainbow balloon with a matching ribbon to the back of each booster chair, to have the children play Color Bingo (available in toy stores), to serve a rainbow cake and to give out T-shirts with rainbows all over them as favors.

Color played a major role in Casey Garr's Purple party when she was two, since purple was her very favorite color. The guests were asked to wear purple, the Jell-O was purple, the grapes were purple, and so were all the decorations. Casey's mom even spray-painted peanuts purple and hid them for a peanut hunt!

Treasure Hunts • Two- and three-year-olds love to hunt for things. There are easy versions of treasure hunts appropriate for these youngsters. Mary Ellen Geisser's party for daughter Carla's third birthday was planned around such a hunt. Mary Ellen wrapped small, inexpensive gifts in different wrapping papers and hid them around the house. Each child was given a scrap of wrapping paper and had to find the matching wrapped gift.

Painting and Coloring • This is the best age for coloring—it's simple to do, and the children love to paint and color in any form. Here's another trick from Mary Ellen. She turned her kitchen into an artist's studio, covering everything with white butcher paper. She then placed cups full of crayons, markers and paints on the floor, and watched the children go to town!

Another version is Zoe Winkler's favorite. Her mother Stacey buys inexpensive white T-shirts and sets up paints in the Winklers' backyard. The children are given plastic aprons and they paint their own T-shirts with acrylic fabric paint tubes and markers. The finished product makes each child very proud of his achievement, and they love taking the shirts home!

Nina Lalli spends hours coloring, so for her birthday party the children wore painted artist aprons. Each child also lay on the floor and had another child trace her shape.

Tools • When Zachary Gordon was nearly three, his favorite activity was playing with tools. He collected toy tools and could often be found hammering away at anything in his room. When it came time for his third birthday, his parents decided to design an entire party around Zachary's passion. They drew a saw and cut it out to use as the invitation. They bought hard hats and gave them out to each guest. Dad Robby made a wooden airplane for each child to paint and arranged pieces of wood on a table in the garage that the children could hammer (since the parents stayed at this party, there was no problem with supervising the children). The best part was when Robby took the backs off a radio, clock and television so the children could look inside and fuss with the inner workings of these "magical" machines. The menu also followed the theme— plastic tools made up the centerpiece, hammer cookie cutters provided "Hammer Sandwiches," and the cake was topped with mini plastic tools.

Animals • What kid doesn't love animals? Not many. Whether they're bears or dinosaurs or kittens, it's easy to build a party around an animal theme (see our Safari party for older children).

Marc Gilbar loved bears when he was three. It didn't matter which kind of bear—Marc loved them all! So for his Bear party Dad Gary bought a white insulation board at his local lumberyard (a 4- by 8-foot sheet cost about $10) and cut out three 10-inch round holes with a mat knife. He then drew three bears, and the other children stuck their heads through the holes and had their pictures taken as "little bears." To carry out the theme, Annie baked a bear cake using a cake pan in the shape of a bear (you can order it from Wilton Enterprises, Inc., 2240 West 75th Street, Woodridge, IL 60517, for approximately $8.50). The children each brought their favorite bear to sit beside them at lunch (they ranged from Winnies

to Paddington to Care Bears) and a family friend read a bear book to the children.

Andrew Herman went to a Dinosaur party when he was three. The children hunted for plastic dinosaurs, made T-shirts with dinosaur rubber stamps and ate cookies in the shapes of the anicent creatures.

Though Jonathan Tucker was only two, he had already amassed a collection of stuffed animals. For his birthday his parents hung the animals on ribbons around the party room. They painted the children's faces as different animals, gave out boxes of animal crackers, and read the book and then watched the movie version of *Curious George*.

Cars • If your son or daughter is a transportation nut, this is a fun party to plan. Decorate the room with all the cars your child owns. (Airplanes, trucks and trains are also great themes!) Since you are inviting only a few children, you can easily make a car from a cardboard box for each child. Take the top off the box, draw wheels or tape paper plates on the sides, tape bottle caps for headlights and ice cream sticks or pencils for windshield wipers. Then just place a child in each car and watch him smile! If you want to go a step further, you can make traffic signs that these youngsters have learned to read. Use paper plates or cut out shapes from construction paper and tape on wooden dowels. STOP, EXIT, YIELD, ONE WAY are all favorites of children this age.

For another travel party that is appropriate for three-, four- and five-year-olds, see our Take A Trip party (page 195).

Balls • Balls, you say? Of course, says J.J. Harvey, Meredith's young second cousin who is obsessed with balls. For his second birthday, the family decided that everything would be "in the round." The food was all circular (cheese balls, round crackers, meatballs, garden peas and a ball-shaped birthday cake served with a scoop of ice cream). They played many games with balls—Nerf balls, rubber balls, Ping-Pong balls, etc. Isn't this a wonderful way to take a simple theme and easily convert it into a party?

Keep It Simple

At ages two and three, a little goes a long way—a little cake, a favorite sandwich, a few games and you're done. Keeping it simple will ensure that your child will remember this early birthday as a happy experience, not an overwhelming and anxious one. The simpler and shorter the party, the less chance you have of unhappiness, tears and anxiety.

Keep It Small

Scale the party to these ages. Don't plan an extravaganza; keep it simple, creative, imaginative and small. Invite two or three children. Having a lot of children at this age gets chaotic and it becomes difficult to keep the attention focused on your child. Give the children small plates, little cups and small portions. Remember, these are very little people! Keep things down to their size and you'll be successful.

Keep It Short

One hour is sufficient time for a party at this age. Any longer and you chance the children getting tired and cranky. Plan the party before or after nap time (10 to 11 a.m. works well, as does 3 to 4 p.m.) to minimize problems with overtired children.

Make It Comfortable

Borrow Sassy and booster seats from friends (or ask the parents to bring theirs) so the children are comfortable and not struggling in adult chairs. You can also rent a children's table with child-size chairs.

Make It Easy

Cover the table with a white paper tablecloth. Place several crayons in paper cups at each place setting. This will keep the children occupied while the cake is served (and for some time after). It will also serve as a pretty tablecloth which can then be folded up and thrown away. Use only paper and plastic utensils. And keep the menu simple. For a short party at this age, all you need is a cake or cupcakes and drinks. Try serving individual cupcakes with candles in them. You will find that all children love the chance to blow out candles!

For a change, have a picnic. Put a plastic tablecloth on the floor and set the table with paper plates and cups. Give each child his lunch in a plastic sand pail. Pretend the children are in a park having a real picnic; they'll soon get into the act and have a ball.

Parents Come and Stay

At this age children are most comfortable with their parents, and you'll find that the parents will stay at the party. This is totally appropriate for this age and will actually make your party easier to handle. Each child will have her parent with her to handle the activities (and to help you).

Easy Games and Activities

Plan simple games. Children at this age don't need elaborate or highly organized games to keep them busy and make them happy. In fact, they are often overwhelmed and frightened by too much activity, too many rules and the presence of a lot of strangers around them. For some two-year-olds, even the benign clown can be scary.

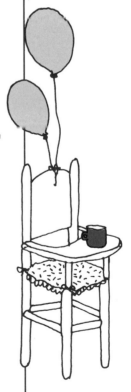

- Besides Treasure Hunts, kids this age love to unwrap things. Try this game: Buy some very inexpensive plastic toys. Wrap one toy in pretty wrapping paper. Now add another toy and wrap the entire package in yet another and different wrapping paper. Now add another gift and wrap the whole thing again. (Be sure you have one gift for each child.) Now have the children sit in a circle. While your child's favorite music is playing, the children pass the package around the circle. When the music stops, the child who is holding the package unwraps it and keeps the gift. The game continues until the last gift is unwrapped. (If the child who gets a gift already has one, have her pass it on to the next child who has not as yet received a package.)
- Young children love to hide. Create a cave by draping a sheet over four chairs placed in a square arrangement. Give each child a flashlight and let the children play in the "cave."

- Any costume party is perfect at this age. Children love to dress up, whether it's pretending to be "grown-ups," which gives them a chance to wear their "dressy" clothes, or coming in a certain costume. There is no reason to wait until Halloween for the kids to wear costumes. Have them dress up to fit your theme and you'll end up with a happy crowd!
- Get balloons of different colors with matching ribbons. Tie the favors at the end of a string and let them hang in the party room. Play some music. When it stops, the children must reach for a balloon.
- Some traditional games are terrific for young children. Old favorites like Hot Potato and Musical Chairs work well because they are easy to explain and to do. Some parents have found that Pin the Tail on anything is not so popular because children this age often don't like to be blindfolded.
- Get some prize ribbons to give out as the children arrive. Appropriate prizes for this age could be: the child with the bluest eyes, the blackest shoes, the longest hair, etc. Getting such a precious ribbon makes each child feel special. Remember to include your birthday child among the winners!
- Make a game out of handing out bibs as young guests arrive. Number the bibs you bought with a permanent marking pen and put them in a basket. Give each guest a number and let him find the matching bib in the basket. These are cute gifts that can also be used by your guests at the party.
- Having the young guests bring some of their toys, particularly as they relate to the theme of the party, is often a good idea. It makes the child feel comfortable when she has one of her own toys with her.
- Any game with music is bound to be a favorite. Sing-along records are always big hits. Encourage the parents to participate as well. If your child has favorite songs, play them. He will feel wonderful at being able to lead the singing. Tape the children singing and play back the tape. The wonderment in their eyes will delight you!
- If your child loves puppets, make or buy some and give a puppet show for your child. It really is easy. Take a favorite book, get the puppets you will need, recruit someone to play puppeteer with you and give your show. The children will hoot and holler. They love puppets and don't need elaborate professional shows to make them happy. Do it yourself and watch the delight in their faces!

Gifts

Opening gifts at this age is exciting but confusing. First of all, waiting to open presents when you are two or three is harder than when you are twelve. Moreover, if the child waits to open her gifts at the end of the party, many children will be tired and cranky—not ideal for gift opening. You might want to have your child open each gift as it arrives with its bearer. This gives your child the chance to take in what she has received; it lets her share her delight with the giver; it enables the giver to see your child's happy face; and it makes the purpose of the party less gift-oriented and more guest-oriented.

Make Your Child Feel Special

Do some extra, simple things to make your child feel that this is his special day. Let him choose things during the day—what he has for breakfast, what he wears. Let him be the "boss." (For example, he can tell you what he wants you to wear for his special day.) Make him a crown and a personal birthday banner, and save both. You can bring it out, year after year, as our friend Nancy Rubin does, and take his picture in the same crown in front of the same banner. Put these pictures, a copy of the invitation, and any thoughts and memories you have after the party in a Birthday Book. Your child may not appreciate this for a few years, but when he is older, these touches will be a truly priceless memory for all of you.

THE PARTIES

Ages 4–12

I t was Pablo Picasso who said, "Every child is an artist. The problem is how to remain an artist once one grows up." This is a party for all the children who may be our future Matisses or Renoirs or Picassos. If your child's passion is art, whether it is painting, puppetry, drawing or printing, collaborate with him on a party he will never forget. Share our ideas with him, then urge him to create his own, and the result will be a party to remember.

1 STAGE ONE

CHECKLIST

1. Discuss artist projects
2. Compile guest list
3. Choose a room for the Artist's Studio
4. Prepare invitation

1. Discuss the various projects your child wants to do at this party. Go over our list of artistic activities, and then add those your child particularly enjoys.

2. Start compiling the guest list.

3. Make sure you have a room in your home that can be conveniently turned into an "Artist's Studio." If you have a recreation room or an empty garage, that's perfect. If you have a playroom where objects can be removed or set aside, that may work as well. Annie's sister, Sonia Ancoli Israel, covered her floor with a plastic tablecloth, which she threw away when the party was over.

4. Prepare the invitation.

INVITATION

The invitation is written on a piece of paper in the shape of a palette that is xeroxed on colored paper and then hand-colored by your child.

Please come to Jenny's
PICASSO PARTY
COME
dressed like an
ARTIST
wear your smock & beret

TIME: _____   PLACE: _____
DATE: _____   R.S.V.P. _____

Now take each invitation and roll it around a 10-inch paint-brush. Place in a padded envelope and mail. For an added touch, have your artist paint the outside of the envelope with acrylics or markers.

STAGE TWO

1. Send the invitations and prepare your RSVP list.

2. Gather the items you will need for the decorations. These include paintbrushes, plastic jars and tubes of paint, paper palettes (which your child can paint) and other products you have or can find in an art store that will create the atmosphere of an artist's studio.

3. Start preparing the activities.
   You will need:

- for all projects: John Adams' Make a Badge Set (or any other button/badge set), cans for water to clean brushes, old rags and/or towels, construction paper, scissors, etc.
- for making T-shirts for the birthday child or, if you and your child prefer, making T-shirts for all the children: the appropriate number of shirts and permanent fabric paint (Euro-Tex or Puff n' Paint, a tube paint that puffs up when ironed) in three or four colors. You can substitute paper painter's hats for the T-shirts.

- for tracing the kids' bodies and for making a mural: a roll of butcher paper, markers, crayons, acrylic paints and brushes
- for making stationery: paper by the pound (ten cards and envelopes for each child), rubber stamps, press-on letters, stickers, ribbons and gift boxes
- for painting pictures the children can take home instead of making stationery (if your child is between four and six years old): paper, crayons and water-soluble markers
- for making sculptures: piles of beads, corks, ribbons, bottle caps, computer paper scraps, scrap wood from a lumberyard, glue, acorns or pinecones, round emery boards, colored cotton balls, sequins, glitter
- for making Froot Loop necklaces: 24-inch shoelaces (one per child) and a couple of boxes of the cereal Froot Loops

CHECKLIST

1. Send invitations
2. Collect decorations
3. Prepare items for activities

33

3 | STAGE THREE

1. Check the guest list and call any RSVPs who haven't responded.

2. Plan your menu. Buy the ingredients now.

3. If you don't have a Polaroid camera, borrow one and make sure you have at least three rolls of film. The Polaroids will be your place cards.

4. Decide on favors for this party. The children will be taking home some of the projects they have made. In addition, you may want to give out sets of markers, artist aprons, small paint sets or any other artist supplies you like.

CHECKLIST

1. Call RSVPs
2. Decide on menu
3. Get Polaroid camera and film
4. Prepare favors

STAGE FOUR

1. Prepare the food. You can make the salad and bake the cake the day before the party. Place the Froot Loops in large plastic bowls so they'll be ready to use for making the necklaces.

2. Set the table. Cover the table with butcher paper. Place the brushes you bought randomly on the table or standing in tall glasses. Strew paint cans, tubes of paint and any other accessories you bought. Place markers and/or crayons in cups at each place setting so the kids can draw to their heart's content while lunch is served.

3. If you have prepared additional favors, get those ready. You might want to get a shopping bag in which each child can carry home his creations.

CHECKLIST

1. Prepare food
2. Set table
3. Get favors ready

ACTIVITIES

Take Polaroid pictures as the children are busy at their various activities. Use each child's picture as a place card at the table. Save the rest for your child's birthday album or to give to the kids to take home. (Sonia took Polaroids as the kids walked in and gave those as favors. She then took another set as the children left, carrying their goodies, and put these in daughter Sarah's birthday album.)

1. T-Shirt Bazaar • The T-shirt–making project can be done in two ways. Either the children make one shirt as a gift for the birthday child or each child makes a shirt for himself. Adjust the activity accordingly. If you are making one T-shirt, place a piece of cardboard inside. Cover the table with newspaper and place three plastic bowls or metal pie tins filled with paint on the table. As each guest arrives, have him put his hand in the paint and press it down for a count of ten. Then have him sign his name with a marker next to his print and wash his hands. (If you've chosen to paint painter's caps, do it now.)

2. Badge Making • Take the badge-making set and have each child make her own badge. Each set has eight badges in it.

3. People Shapes • Place large sheets of butcher paper on the floor. Have each child take turns lying down on the paper as another child makes an outline of his body. Cut the paper at the end of the outline and hang it up. The children can take these home. If they want, they can also draw in their faces and clothes. When they are done, take a picture of each child with his outline.

4. Birthday Banner • Again using butcher paper, make a birthday banner. Assign each child a "Happy Birthday" letter and have him decorate it with markers and/or glitter.

5. Stationery Factory • Children love to make their own stationery (using it is another story!). Take the paper by the pound and give each child ten pieces and ten envelopes. Give her rubber stamps, stickers, markers and press-on letters (you may have to show young children how these work). Have ribbons on hand to tie around the stationery. If you have gift boxes, that's even nicer!

6. Sculptures • On a large table, pile everything you bought to create sculptures—pieces of wood, beads, glitter, corks, ice cream sticks, colored cotton balls and buttons, ribbons and any other items of your imagination. Make sure you have enough glue, scissors, markers, pliers, string and twine. The rules are easy—the children create their own sculptures.

7. Froot Loop Necklaces • When you set the table for lunch, place the Froot Loops in the bowls on the table and strew the shoelaces between these bowls. As the children sit down, they can make necklaces while the food is being served.

8. LUNCH

M • E • N • U

Painter's Pasta Salad
with
Bread Sticks

Picasso Cake

Suzanne Turman gave an art party for her son Peter. She borrowed easels from all her friends so each child could have his own. She also asked the children to come dressed in Dad's old huge shirts so they could be comfortable painting.

TIP

For a different invitation, use a blank credit card form, airplane ticket, bank deposit slip or calendar page, and fill out with the party information.

See the recipes on page 216.

FAVORS

The children take home the things they have made—T-shirts, badges, sculptures, body outlines and stationery. If you bought extra favors, like marker sets or other artist supplies, give them out at the end of the party. A nice touch is to have a personalized shopping bag with a ribbon for each child to fill with her art creations. Additional appropriate favors are the books *Norman the Doorman* by Don Freeman and *Bear's Picture* by Daniel Pinkwater.

✳ Hilly Ripmaster, from Birmingham, Michigan, left a pan of acrylic fabric paint at the front door. As the guests arrived, each dipped his hand in the paint and placed it on one white T-shirt. The kids then signed their names with permanent magic markers next to their prints (and then washed their hands in the bathroom sink). On the top of the shirt, Hilly wrote, "Happy Birthday From A Handful Of Friends"— a wonderful gift for the birthday child. For a twist on the theme, do footprints and sign the shirt, "Happy Birthday From Toes of Us Who Love You!"

WELCOME! TO SCHOOL

HURRAH! SCHOOL IS OUT!

SUNTAN OIL

1987 Summer

BACK TO SCHOOL

OR

SCHOOL IS OUT PARTY

Ages 5–12

T here are two versions of this party. Your child can celebrate the end of the school year or the beginning of a new one. Both celebrations are emotional and exciting. At the end of the year, there is a sadness at leaving many school friends for the summer months; and at the start of the new year, there is an excitement at seeing everyone again, at anticipating what the new year will hold, and a thrill at catching up with everyone's summer stories.

You may find that you don't need to plan as much for this party as for others. Most children, the older ones particularly (those eight and older), will most likely be eager to share their experiences and thoughts, and thus will want to have time to themselves. Scheduling a meal and some light activities is best. For the younger children, we have added additional games to keep them busy and happy.

1 STAGE ONE

1. Prepare invitation.

INVITATION

At the stationery store, buy blank forms to fill out with the party information. For the Back to School party, get an inexpensive calendar, tear out September and mark the day of the party. Write the information on that day and xerox for each guest. Your child can color in that day on each calendar page.

CHECKLIST

1. Prepare guest list; make and send out the invitations
2. Compile things you will need for games and activities
3. Buy decorations
4. Buy favors

SEPTEMBER

COME TO JESSICA'S
BACK TO SCHOOL BASH
« TODAY »
2:00 pm UNTIL 5:00 pm
AT
15564 Strawberry Lane
Bring Pictures of Your
Fabulous Summer!
PLEASE SAY YES! 555-1234 •

You can use the same invitation for a School Is Out party, or design a Report Card where everyone got A's in activities like watching television, signing yearbooks, saying good-byes, planning trips and promising to write; the invitation is written on top. Then buy plastic sunglasses and tie the invitations to them.

REPORT CARD	
WATCHING TV	A+
SKATEBOARDING	A+
SWIMMING	A+
BIKING	A+
SOFT BALL	A+
POOL PARTIES	A+

2. Buy items for games and activities. Get blank certificate awards at a stationery store. Get camera and film for group pictures. For the School Is Out party, buy paper by the pound, stickers, rubber stamps, markers and press-on letters so the kids can make stationery. For the Back to School party, get individual photo albums or address books the children can decorate, plus tape, buttons, sequins, lace, ribbons and press-on letters. Buy inexpensive T-shirts and fabric paints for both parties.

3. Prepare the decorations. For the Back to School party, gather random stationery items (notebooks, reading books, pencils galore, erasers, memo pads, reminder notes, etc.). You can put these in a pile at the center of the table. For the School Is Out party, get some or all of the following and place in the center of the table: sunglasses, suntan lotion bottles, paperback books or comics, travel folders, plastic toy cameras, and any other items you and your child think would humorously represent summer vacation. (You can make the favors part of the centerpiece as well.)

4. As favors buy individual address books for the School Is Out party (autograph books also work well), a book of stamps and/or an unusual travel-size pen. A small collection of school supplies is perfect for the Back to School party. If you plan the party at least four weeks ahead, you will have time to order personalized pencils for each guest. (Write to Seastrom Associates, 133 West 19th Street, New York, NY 10011, [212] 243-1488.)

2 STAGE TWO

CHECKLIST

1. Buy and make food
2. Make banner and signs
3. Gather favors
4. Set table

1. Check the menu and buy food items (drinks and ice cream), order pizza, and bake the Chocolate Mint Cookies. If this is a birthday party, choose a cake from our menus and bake it today. If you bake a sheet cake, an appropriate topping might be a lake (blue icing with plastic fish and a boat) for the School Is Out party. For the Back to School party, bake a sheet cake and draw a ruler with icing in a tube or cover the cake with plastic rulers.

2. Make a banner saying either "Hurrah! School Is Out" or "Welcome Back to School" and hang it over the front door. You can make other signs with famous sayings to hang around the party room.

3. Gather the favors in one place so they'll be easy to give out.

4. Set the table. Decorate it with the items you bought. They work well in the center of the table as a centerpiece.

"THE BEST WAY TO MAKE CHILDREN GOOD IS TO MAKE THEM HAPPY."
— Oscar Wilde

"NO MORE LESSONS, NO MORE BOOKS NO MORE TEACHER'S SASSY LOOKS, NO MORE LATIN, NO MORE FRENCH, NO MORE SITTING ON THE BENCH."

"A LITTLE LEARNING IS A DANGEROUS THING, BUT NONE AT ALL IS FATAL."
— Viscount Samuel

"IT IS WHAT WE THINK WE KNOW ALREADY THAT OFTEN PREVENTS US FROM LEARNING."
— Claude Bernard

"A LEARNED MAN IS AN IDLER WHO KILLS TIME BY STUDY."
— George Bernard Shaw

"NO MAN NEEDS A VACATION SO MUCH AS THE PERSON WHO HAS JUST HAD ONE."
— Elbert Hubbard

"IT USED TO TAKE ME ALL VACATION TO GROW A NEW HIDE IN PLACE OF THE ONE THEY FLOGGED OFF ME DURING THE SCHOOL TERM"
— Mark Twain

ACTIVITIES

These are hands-on activities. If your child wants to also play games, you can choose any games from the other parties.

1. Sharing Experiences • The children will have a lot to talk about and share at both of these parties. If you think they need some assistance in getting started, you could encourage them to talk about their summer experiences or those of the past school year. If you have a video camera, you can tape their conversations and then play them back.

2. Group Photo • No matter which party you are giving, take a group picture of the kids. You or your child can send it to them later, either at camp or vacation or at home if they are starting school.

3. Awards • Remember those certificates you bought? This is the time to have the children vote on who wins them and for what. Some suggestions for the Back to School party include: the deepest tan; no tan; longest hair; who grew the most; the shortest hair; the funniest story; the farthest trip—and add more of your own. For the School Is Out party, how about: the one who is traveling the farthest; the one who worked hardest; the one who watched the most television; the one who got away with the most; the best at sports; the funniest; the best speller—and your own additions.

4. Notepads or Address Books • With the paper, rubber stamps and press-on letters, have the children make notepads for school. If you have bought address books for the School Is Out party, have them decorate and/or personalize the covers.

5. Photo Albums • Children at both parties would love photo albums. Get inexpensive ones with covers that can be accessorized. Gather the glue, scissors, tape, press-on letters and other paraphernalia and let them go to it!

6. T-Shirts • You can paint the shirts in school colors or in any summery design. You can use the fabric paints and markers for the design and then glue or sew any other objects the children like. Some fabulous T-shirts have plastic charms sewn to them.

7. LUNCH

M • E • N • U

Pizza

Drinks and/or Ice Cream Sodas

Chocolate Mint Cookies

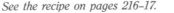

FAVORS

At the Back to School party, give out the stationery items and/or personalized pencils. At the School Is Out party, the address book, book of stamps and pens are the favors. At both parties the children take home all the things they have made.

✳ Janice Treadwell's favorite Back to School party was a black and white affair. The invitations were crossword puzzles, the guests wore black and white (some came in white face), the decorations were lots of black and white balloons, the cake was decorated with black licorice, and the children held a mime theater.

Thought you'd overplanned but found that you still need a last-minute activity? Try an impromptu talent show which needs no advance planning. Announce that it is time for the show and you're bound to get a cartwheeler, a rendition of "Old MacDonald," a ballerina who is eager to demonstrate her turns, and more. The kids will sit glued in place while the entertainment is going on.

See the recipe on pages 216–17.

BACKWARDS
YTЯAꟼ

Ages 4–12

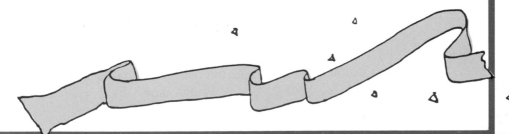

Just hearing the words "Backwards Party" will set the funny, frivolous, joyful mood for this party. When the children get the invitation they will immediately start planning their costumes and look forward with great anticipation to the fun that lies ahead. The mood is set by the invitation, and is continued with the decorations and activities around this lovably silly theme.

1 | STAGE ONE

1. Decide on your invitation and the number of children you will have.

INVITATION

Write out, or trace over, this invitation with a thick, felt-tipped pen and then xerox it.

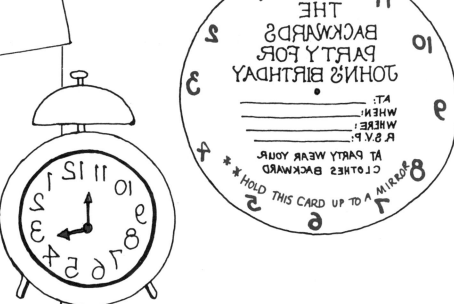

CHECKLIST

1. Prepare invitation and make up guest list
2. Discuss backwards theme

Do not address the envelope backwards: the letter carrier will not think this is funny.

2. Talk to your child about the various possibilities of where to have the party (in the backyard, in your living room or playroom, at grandmother's house, etc.). Ask him for his ideas of activities and designs in the backwards theme. Make this the topic of conversation for the next couple of weeks so the whole family can get into the backwards theme. Start making lists of everyone's ideas.

STAGE TWO

1. Send out the invitations and make out the guest list for the RSVPs.

2. Collect, make and/or buy:

> place cards
> balloons
> paper plates, cups, napkins, etc.
> ribbons, beans, paper and pens, and stuffed animals for relay
> questions and answers for Lib Ad game
> bucket or pail and wooden clothespins for the Shoulder Toss
> a copy of our Find the Mistakes drawing, one copy per child (and make some extras!)
> a list of words for the Backwards Spelling Bee
> the favors

CHECKLIST

1. Send out invitations
2. Collect and buy accessories

STAGE THREE

1. Check the RSVP list. Call anyone who has not yet responded.

2. Make arrangements for extra help. Find a couple of high school kids who want to help. Talk to them about the party ahead of time, outlining your expectations and giving them the details of the party.

3. Gather the ingredients for your lunch. If you would feel more secure, try baking the Ugly Chocolate Birthday Cake, not so much to test it, because we already have, but to make sure your child likes the way it looks.

4. As soon as you have the completed guest list, make out the place cards by writing the names backwards (you'll be facing the cards the wrong way on the table).

5. Buy inexpensive T-shirts, fabric acrylic paint and several sets of letter stencils.

6. Make a birthday banner to hang on the front door and spell the words backwards.

CHECKLIST

1. Check on RSVPs
2. Arrange extra help
3. Gather ingredients for menu
4. Make place cards
5. Buy T-shirts, paint and letter stencils
6. Make birthday banner

4 STAGE FOUR

1. Buy the hamburger meat or hot dogs, buns, and potato chips.

2. Bake the Ugly Chocolate Birthday Cake and refrigerate.

3. Set the table to be as graphically and obviously backwards as you can. Put those place cards backwards (facing the inside of the table). Put the plates and cups upside down. Mix up and turn over the forks and spoons.

4. Hang the backwards birthday banner on the front door.

Assemble the balloons and sticks so you can blow them up in the morning and set them around the room hanging upside down.

Do whatever else you can think of—that is comfortable and not dangerous—to create a backwards, fun-filled atmosphere. For example, you can place the chairs backwards, turn any pillows around facing the wrong way, turn paintings or photographs facing the wall—go to it. This is the time to be creatively silly. The children will really love this extra effort.

5. Check the games list and prepare whatever you need (with extras on hand so you won't run out of anything).

CHECKLIST

1. Buy food
2. Bake cake
3. Set table
4. Decorate
5. Prepare for games

ACTIVITIES

1. T-Shirt Decoration • Have the table prepared with paper cover, paints, T-shirts and stencils. Let each guest begin working on a shirt when he arrives at the party. Having one shirt done ahead of time gives everyone an idea of how to proceed.

2. Reverse Relay • Now divide all the children into two teams for the entire party. You can choose two colors: for example, Red is Der and Yellow is Wolley and you call them by these names. Tie the red ribbons around each child's arm on one team, and do the same with the yellow for the other team. In this way both teams will be easily identifiable. (Be sure you have enough ribbons in each color for each child.) Now you're ready to play the games:

The object is to do (a) and (b) with your left hand (left-handed people must do it with their right hand). The first person on each team does all three activities and then the next person follows. The first team to finish wins.

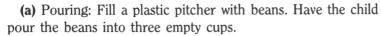

(a) Pouring: Fill a plastic pitcher with beans. Have the child pour the beans into three empty cups.

(b) Writing: For six-year-olds and up, have the child write Happy Birthday backwards. For four- to five-year-olds, have them write a letter backwards. (If this is too difficult, just have them write their name with their left hand if they are right-handed and with their right hand if they are left-handed.)

(c) Place two stuffed animals on the table, surrounded by clothes that fit them. Have the child dress the animal backwards and then take the clothes off and replace them on the table.

3. Lib Ad Game, or "You Are Who?" • This question and answer game is good for ages seven to ten.

You need to prepare ten questions on a piece of paper (or you can use ours). Keep these for your eyes only. Give everyone paper and pencil and ask them to number from 1 to 10 (or you can do this before and xerox). Now ask the children the first set of questions below and have them write down the answers. When this is done, read them the second set of questions and have them each read their answers. Nothing will match and the results will be hilarious for them and you.

Ask them to answer the following questions:

1. Name a planet.
2. What is your favorite color?
3. Pick a number from 1 to 50.
4. Who is your favorite cartoon character?
5. Name a famous person (girls pick a male, boys pick a female).
6. Write the weirdest career you can think of.
7. Write a number from 20 to 1000.
8. What is your favorite car?
9. Which vegetable do you dislike?
10. What have you broken lately?

Now read the children the following questions and have them read their answers, each in turn:

1. Where were you born?
2. What color are your eyes?
3. How old are you today?
4. What's your teacher's name?
5. Whom will you marry?
6. What business will you be in when you grow up?
7. How many kids will you have?
8. Where will you live when you grow up?
9. What's your favorite dessert?
10. What's your favorite birthday gift?

4. Shoulder Toss • This is good for ages four to six, although even older kids find this silly game a challenge.

Place a bucket or pail on the floor and have a dish full of wooden clothespins. Have each member of each team stand in front of the bucket with his back to it and hand him the clothespins. The object is to throw the clothespins, one at a time, over his shoulder and get them into the bucket. The team with the most clothespins in the bucket wins. (Just add the total number of pins each child got into the bucket.)

5. Find the Mistakes • Xerox the drawing on page 44 or have it blown up to a larger size. Select a team captain for each of the red and yellow teams (one could be the birthday child) and give her a colored pencil. Set a kitchen timer to an appropriate time (you can gauge the attention span of your age group). Tell the children that there are twenty backwards mistakes in this drawing and each team must find all the mistakes. The first team to do so wins.

6. Backwards Spelling Bee • Appropriate for ages seven to ten. Take the list of spelling words you compiled last week. Have the teams spell the words backwards. Make them fairly simple (four to five letters at the most), since this is harder than you may think!

TIP

As the guests come up to the door or up your walkway, make them walk backwards and greet the birthday child backwards. Instead of piling the gifts on a table, stack them under a table or chair.

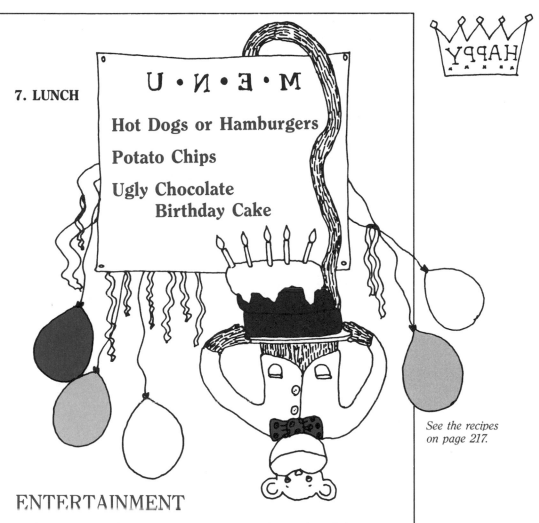

7. LUNCH

M • E • N • U

Hot Dogs or Hamburgers

Potato Chips

Ugly Chocolate
Birthday Cake

*See the recipes
on page 217.*

ENTERTAINMENT

If you want to have a quiet moment in the midst of the excitement, a good book to read with younger children is *Wacky Wednesday*.

FAVORS

The T-shirts are the favors. If you haven't included this activity, you might choose books to give as favors. *Wacky Wednesday* by Theodore Le Sieg, *Alexander and the Terrible, Horrible, No Good Very Bad Day* by Judith Viorst, and *Upside Down Day* by Mike Thaler are good thematically.

✱ When Hope Miller had her Backwards party, she was really surprised by a couple of guests who approached the front door backwards and asked *her* for birthday presents.

BACKYARD BEACH PARTY

Ages 4 and up

Y ou do not have to have a backyard pool for this party. For children, running around under the sprinklers can sometimes be even more fun than swimming. How many of us remember the sounds of giggling and shrieking youngsters as they run in and around the spraying hose, laughing at the squirting water and loving every minute of it? Multiply that by the sound of a dozen happy and wet children running around your backyard having the time of their lives and you have the makings of a Backyard Beach party.

1 | STAGE ONE

1. Decide how many children will be invited to this party. You can easily handle twelve to sixteen children if you have the room in your backyard and enough adult supervision. The games are designed for many children, and the picnic lunch is easy to stretch. The great thing about this party is that different ages can participate in all the activities. If this is a birthday party, inviting younger or older relatives will not disturb the activities. There are enough different things to do so that everyone can have fun.

2. Buy one plastic shovel per guest—that is the invitation.

3. Make and send the invitations.

INVITATION

Buy large labels that will fit on the face of the shovels. You can write the invitation on each label or type it and have it copied at your local copier store. You can also write directly on the plastic shovel with a permanent marker. The invitation could read:

COME TO LARSON'S BACKYARD BEACH PARTY
bring a bathing suit ☆ and a towel
(be prepared to get wet)
DATE: _____
TIME: _____
PLACE: _____
R.S.V.P. 555-1245

JANE BROWN
MAIN STREET
CONN. USA
Beach

Now glue each label on the face of each shovel and mail in a padded envelope (or deliver them, if you can). On the outside, with a thick marking pen or a tube of paint, make a large "B" and write the address in the letter. Add the letters "each" in lower case to form the word "Beach" along the bottom of the envelope. Send the invitations and wait for the happy replies.

STAGE TWO 2

This is the time to start buying and collecting all the things you will need for the activities.

1. You will need four or five plastic wading pools (they are quite inexpensive). If you can borrow any, do so. Three or four of these will be filled with water. The other one or two will be filled with sand. (You choose—if your child likes the water games more than the sand games, have only one "sand pool" and three "water pools.") You can buy sand at a lumberyard or nursery.

2. Buy lots of balloons and store in a safe place (safe means away from the children—balloons have a notoriously short life span when around children).

3. Buy one pail per child, you will be serving lunch in these pails. They will also hold the favors, which can include wind-up toys, pinwheels, soap bubbles and pipes for the younger children; sunglasses, visors and colored sunblock tubes for the older ones. If you give the visors as favors, you can also buy markers to write each child's name on them.

4. You will need lots of sand toys. Borrow as many as you can (write the owner's name on the toy with a marker so it will be easy to return later) and buy the ones you can't borrow. And, of course, the more toys, the merrier. Having lots of the same toy only prevents problems with children who want the toy someone else has. The best are pails, sifters, shovels, water wheels, molds, sponges (in different shapes), vacuum pumps, squirt toys, wind-up toys, water guns, plastic containers, even soup ladles and basters. Get as many different bubble pipes and horns (and any other toys that make bubbles) as you can. Get at least two small hula hoops (about 24 inches).

5. Get a hose or two. If you have any attachments that create designs with the water, use them. They are fun for the children to run through.

You will need Styrofoam cups, water pistols, aerosol shaving cream and serrated plastic knives for the games.

CHECKLIST

1. Buy or borrow wading pools
2. Buy balloons
3. Buy plastic pails and/or other favors
4. Borrow or buy sand toys
5. Get hoses and other accessories

3

STAGE THREE

1. Call any people who have not responded.

2. If you would like to personalize the lunch pails, do it now that you have your final guest list. Write each child's name with a permanent marker on the pail. You can do this in different colors and have your child add any design for added fun.

3. Check the above list to see if there is anything you still have to buy for the games.

4. Make arrangements to borrow extra beach towels the day before the party. You want to have lots of those around!

5. Check your menu. This is the time to decide on everything you want in your picnic lunch.

6. This party is held outdoors so you won't need any decorations, although you may want to make a birthday banner to hang over the front door or the gate to your backyard. You won't need to set a table either, because lunch will be served in pails outside.

7. For Bubble Heaven you will need a bottle of Joy dish washing liquid soap and a bottle of glycerine. Wait until you see those bubbles!

CHECKLIST

1. Call RSVPs
2. Personalize lunch pails
3. Buy any accessories for games
4. Gather beach towels
5. Check menu
6. Make birthday banner
7. Get Joy soap and glycerine

4

STAGE FOUR

1. This is the time to go to the market. You will need: the ingredients for Tyler's Little Drummers, including chicken drummettes (that's the part of the wing that looks like a little chicken leg; you can ask your butcher to pack them for you, figuring on two per child), Thumb Print Cookies and Swimming Pool Birthday Cake, as well as carrots and individual bags of potato chips. Get lots of drinks; the easiest thing to do is to make gallons of lemonade or punch. Get at least three times the number of paper cups as people.

2. Bake the birthday cake and Thumb Print Cookies. Make the chicken drummettes and refrigerate.

CHECKLIST

1. Buy food
2. Bake cake and cookies
3. Prepare plastic pools
4. Gather water toys, pails and towels
5. Package favors

3. Set out the plastic pools. Fill one or two with sand and hide the wind-up toys in it. Fill the others with water. (For older children you can hide pennies in the sand.)

4. Gather all the water toys together in large garbage bags and set outside in one place. Pile the personalized plastic pails for the lunches in a corner of the kitchen. Prepare extra beach towels.

5. The children will get the pails and visors as favors. If you are planning to fill the pails with other goodies instead, package these goodies in plastic bags so they will be ready to be put into the pails when the party is nearly over. (Don't forget—these are the same pails that will carry the lunch, so they can't be filled with favors ahead of time.)

ACTIVITIES

As our friend Nancy Rubin says, "At any party that's held outside, there's never enough time! At any party that's held inside, there always seems to be more than enough time!" That's why we have what will seem like a lot of activities for this outdoor party. But be aware that you don't have to do all of them. It is better to have more possibilities than to get caught with time on your hands (although, if you do have extra time, the children will always invent something to do with the water and hoses).

As the children arrive at the yard, hand them the visors with their names on them and get them started with some of the sand toys. This will keep them busy until all the children arrive and the games start.

1. Stomping or Tossing Water Balloons • Have an adult fill some balloons with water from the hose outside. For younger children, the most fun they can have is to simply stomp on the balloons. The only trouble is you will have to have a lot of water-filled balloons handy. For older children, divide them into two teams. The object is to toss the balloon to a teammate without breaking it. Keep going until all the children have had several turns. When all the balloons have burst, the game is over.

✳ Jed Weitzman's favorite movie was *Animal House*, so for his birthday he begged for a whipped cream fight. The kids got together by the pool and had a terrific whipped cream hullabaloo. When they were done, they merely got hosed off.

TIP

Pam Rafanowicz has made bubble solutions for her kids many times. She mixes 1 cup water, 1 cup liquid Joy detergent and 1 cup glycerine (available at drugstores). She puts this solution on a cookie sheet (the kind with a lip) and bends wire coat hangers so they form a closed circle. She then dips the wire circle in the mixture and slowly pulls it out at an angle and waves it through the air, giving her wrist a flick to release the super giant bubble.

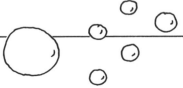

You can give a Beach party in the winter in your home. Serve lunch at an indoor picnic, rent green Astroturf at a party rental store, have the kids bring shorts, put sandwiches in sand pails, blow up beach balls and other inflatables and place around the house, hand each guest a beach towel to sit on for games and lunch, organize a treasure hunt with a beach theme. This is especially entertaining for housebound kids.

✳ For people with pools: Ira Reiner and Diane Wayne love water—Diane used to teach swimming. One year, for daughter Annie's seventh birthday, they hired a swimming teacher to teach the kids water ballet. All the guests spent the first part of the party learning to perform a water ballet (those who couldn't swim were given life jackets). When the parents arrived, they were surprised by the children performing an actual water ballet.

For their eight-year-old son Tommy, the Reiners asked a funny friend of theirs, who loves to perform, to do water antics with the children. He dressed in an outrageous bathing suit, jumped in the water pretending to be a clown and otherwise spent the time being totally silly with the children.

2. Sandbox Surprises • Lead the children to the sandbox where the wind-up toys (or pennies if the kids are older) are hidden. They need to find them all. After they have all been found (you should have hidden about three toys per child, so that will give you a hint as to how many toys there are), put them in one of the pools of water and watch all the toys go at once.

3. Spray Shoot • Line up an arcade of Styrofoam cups along a tabletop, fence or some such stable area. Stand the children in a row about four to eight feet away, depending on the age and size of the child. Give the first child a water pistol and let him try to shoot the cups down. He gets two tries, and gets to go again if he misses both. When done, send him to the back of the line and continue. (Meredith's sister, Leslie Larson, uses a variation of this game. Her kids like to fasten pinwheels and shoot them with water to make them turn. This is harder, but will be a challenge for older children.)

4. Quick Shave • Blow up one balloon per child. Give each child a can of shaving cream so that she can cover the balloon with the cream. Now hand the kids plastic knives and ask them to shave the balloon. The first one to have a clean balloon wins. When done, you can suggest to the kids that they put shaving cream on one another. Just watch their faces as they digest this information ("Are they serious? We're allowed to do this forbidden thing?"). Then run and get your camera. The photos will bring smiles to your faces for years to come.

5. Sprinkler Sillies • If you did find any of those attachments for your hose—the ones that spray water in pretty designs—this is the time to turn them on. Have the children run through them and enjoy the fun. You can ask the children to act out silly faces and dances—or just let them use their imagination running through the streams of water.

6. Bubble Heaven • Pour 1 cup Joy and 1 cup glycerine into each of the plastic pools, which have been filled with 2 inches of water. This will make a wonderful soap bubble solution. Put a hula hoop in each pool. Have each child take a turn pulling the hoop out of the pool and forming an enormous bubble—one large enough to put over the child's head. You can also gather a variety of bubble pipes to create a soap bubble heaven. Toy stores also carry wands that produce big bubbles.

7. LUNCH

S. S. PENNY

M • E • N • U

Tyler's Little Drummers
Carrot Sticks
Bags of Potato Chips
Thumb Print Cookies
Swimming Pool
Birthday Cake

WHISTLE

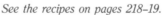

happy birthday

See the recipes on pages 218–19.

FAVORS

The favors are the personalized pails and sun visors. As we mentioned earlier, you can also fill the pails with wind-up toys, pinwheels, sand toys, sunglasses or soap bubbles and pipes. As the children are drying off and calming down, have the adults fill the pails with those extra toys (they can also collect some of the many wind-ups and squirting toys that are by now scattered around the yard—and give those away, too).

When Leslie Larson moved into her new home in Albuquerque, New Mexico, she found the move a difficult one for her young children. We suggested Leslie plan a Backyard Beach party for Josh and Jessie to meet the kids in the neighborhood. Leslie reported that, at first, the neighbors were stunned when the three of them rang doorbells delivering "shovel" invitations. The kids got very involved in decorating the yard; they hung pictures of sea life on a huge net, gathered the sand toys and made bubbles, and had a ball even before the party came around. The resulting smash made the kids an instant hit in their new neighborhood—and Leslie has had to promise to make this an annual event!

BALLET PARTY

Ages 4–8

A h! The ballet! Is there a little girl who hasn't dreamed of dancing in a fluffy tutu, crown on her head, pink satin ballet shoes on
her toes? Ballet and ballerinas have always held a certain mystique
for young girls. If your daughter shares the fantasy of being a
ballerina, a Ballet party will make her dreams come true.

1 STAGE ONE

1. Make up your guest list and prepare the invitations.

INVITATION

Xerox or copy the ballet slipper below. Cut out the holes as drawn. Buy ¼-inch satin ribbon and cut into 16-inch lengths. Thread the ribbon through the holes on the ballet shoe and tie in a pretty bow at the "ankle." Fill in the information on the invitation.

CHECKLIST

1. Make up guest list and prepare invitations
2. Make tutus
3. Hire a dancer
4. Prepare favors
5. Get music

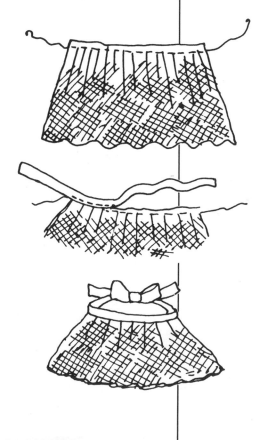

HOLE

please join
CAILA
in a performance
of the ballet
SWAN LAKE
on her Birthday
♦ ♦ ♦ ♦
SATURDAY, NOV. 19TH
FROM 1 TO 3 PM

WEAR LEOTARD & TIGHTS
performance for Parents
at 2:30 PM
555 ORIOLE CANYON
R.S.V.P. 555-6677

2. This is the time to plan making the tutus for the girls. It is really a simple task. You will need one yard of 72-inch wide netting (it usually costs less than a dollar a yard) for every two tutus, lace ribbon for trim, and needle and thread. Simply gather one edge of the netting with a long basting stitch by hand or machine—tie loosely at the end to make it adjustable—and that's it. You can sew on the lace ribbon as a trim. It is really simple, but if you have a large number to do, ask a grandmother or neighbor to help. You can make them all one color or multicolored. Since the girls have been invited to wear tights and leotards, simply tie the tutus on them as they arrive. Within minutes you will have an entire corps de ballet.

3. Find a local dance student (present or former) who can come to the party, tell the story of the ballet, and teach the children some basic ballet steps. The music of *Swan Lake* or *The Nutcracker Suite* is perfect. Discuss with her your plans to have the children perform a small ballet at the end of the party.

4. Arrange for the favors. Of course, the tutus are favors, but you can also include tiaras, crowns or boas (which the girls can wear at the performance). The story of *Swan Lake* or *The Nutcracker Suite* is a wonderful memory of the party, either in a book or record.

5. Make sure you have the appropriate recorded music for the performance, whether it is *Swan Lake* or any other ballet.

STAGE TWO 2

1. Call any RSVPs. You may need to remind the guests to wear tights and leotards.

2. It is really wonderful to videotape this party, both the learning part and the actual performance. If at all possible, borrow or rent a camera. You will find that this tape will be watched again and again!

3. Set the menu. You can plan a lunch to be eaten after the performance or have a Celebration Tea instead. If the party starts at 1 p.m., chances are the children have already had

CHECKLIST

1. Call RSVPs
2. Line up a video camera
3. Set menu
4. Decide and prepare decorations

lunch. By the time they give their performance, they'll be ready for what is basically birthday cake and drinks.

4. You will want to decorate the table for a "fancy tea." Set the table with a paper "lace" cloth and lots of doilies. Use flowered paper plates and cups. Real flowers for the centerpiece are lovely. Favors can be put at each place setting. If the children are performing *Swan Lake*, you might place some small plastic swans around the table. Miniature toy nutcrackers work for you-know-what. You can also find plastic ballerinas in shops that sell cake decorations.

With your child, make a large sign announcing the performance. Write the words "Corps de Ballet" and list each guest's name. If you like, you can write "Starring" and use your child's name. Make a program including each child's name and xerox copies. Giving the program out when the parents arrive is a great task to assign to a sibling.

Music can play an important role at the party. Use it to set the mood (*Space Odyssey* for the astronauts, eerie melodies for the ghosts, patriotic themes or marches for the Olympic party, ballet or orchestral music for the Ballet party) or as background for games and activities.

3 STAGE THREE

1. Set the table and decorate it now so you won't have to do it tomorrow. You may want to add fresh flowers to make the "tea" seem more grown-up.

2. Turn the party room into a theater and stage. Decide where the stage area will be and where the audience can observe. Don't worry about seating everyone—the performance won't be that long! No curtains or exit signs needed, either.

3. Bake the cake, decorate and refrigerate it.

4. Arrange the favors either in individual packages or on the table at each place setting.

CHECKLIST

1. Set the table and decorate
2. Make a theater in the party room
3. Bake cake
4. Prepare favors

ACTIVITIES

1. Making Tutus • If your girls are ages four to eight, you have made the tutus for them; put them on the girls as they arrive. For girls from eight to eleven, have them make the tutus at the party. Organize this as an activity; they'll enjoy it, and when they're done, you can go on to the main show.

2. The Ballet • *The* activity at this party is to learn the dance steps and then perform the ballet. By this time everything should be set—the theater is created, the programs have been made, the costumes are ready, the cameraman is standing by, and the ballet is ready to begin.

3. LUNCH

M • E • N • U

Lemonade or
Sparkling Cider
Aunt Cora's Cake
Ice Cream

See the recipes on pages 219–20.

FAVORS

The tutus, and possibly the tiaras, are the main favors. As we mentioned, ballet books are wonderful mementos of the party. Any ballet-related items would be appropriate.

✻ Marie Evans hired a dancer from the Joffrey Ballet to tell the story of *Swan Lake* and help the children act it out. And the little boy who came dressed as the hunter, complete with a bow and arrow, was a great hit!

BASEBALL PARTY

Ages 6–12

[M] ention baseball to a group of boys (and sometimes girls) and you are guaranteed to see their faces light up. Baseball holds out the promise of team spirit, winning, cheering, hot dogs and popcorn, and nonstop fun. You can give your child a party that will let him experience the spirit of baseball firsthand—and you don't have to have a baseball diamond in your backyard to do it. Our Baseball party combines the flavor of baseball with some inventiveness of our own.

1 STAGE ONE

1. For this invitation you may need as much as three months' planning. Seastrom Associates in New York will make personalized baseball cards with your child's picture on them (plus his "statistics" on the back). Once you decide on a Baseball party, contact this company, send them a photo (preferably a head shot) of your child and sit back and wait for the cards to arrive. They will be used as the invitation. The cost of fifty cards is approximately $36. (Write to Seastrom Associates, 133 West 19th Street, New York, NY 10011. Delivery time: 5–6 weeks.)

You can choose what information you want to appear on the other side. You have two options: One is to merely give your child's statistical information (date of birth, height, weight, etc.) and then attach a piece of paper with the party information over the back of the card; the other is to give the party information (date, place, time, RSVP number, dress in uniform, etc.) on the reverse side of the photo. This will result in a completed invitation when you receive the cards. Of course, chances are you won't be needing fifty invitations, but you can use the extra for place cards or party decorations.

CHECKLIST

1. Prepare invitation

PENNY WHISTLE

MARC GILBAR

PENNY WHISTLE

COME TO
MARC GILBAR's
Baseball Party

DATE: _____
PLACE: _____
RSVP _____

DRESS IN UNIFORM *

game time: 10:30

* bring your own mitt

SHORTSTOP
MARC GILBAR

If, however, you have decided to give the Baseball party a month or so before the actual date and don't have the time to have the baseball cards made, merely xerox the illustration of a baseball card on this page and duplicate as many photographs of your son in a baseball getup as you need invitations. Now cut out the marked space on our baseball card and insert a photograph of your son in each of these invitations. Write the pertinent information on the back and you're set.

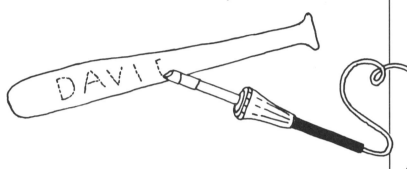

STAGE TWO 2

1. Send out the invitations and make up the RSVP list.

2. Buy a wood-burning kit if you want to write each child's name on a wooden baseball bat.

3. Buy baseball cards to be used for Baseball Bingo. Collect 8×11-inch cardboard sheets (you can use cardboard that comes in men's shirts), one for each guest, and glue sixteen cards on each piece (four across, four down). This will be the basis of your bingo game. Get extra cards to match the bingo cards (you will use these to call out the cards) and poker chips or pennies to cover the card in the game.

4. Get baseball hats of your local teams or your child's favorite team to hand out as guests arrive.

5. Either buy a Baseball Trivia Game or make one up with any baseball expert you can find.

6. You can order rubber baseball figures for your cake from Wilton Enterprises, Inc., 2240 West 75th Street, Woodridge, IL 60517. The following will look terrific on the Baseball Diamond Cake: Baseball Set (includes batter, catcher, pitcher and three basemen), #2113-2155; a Little Leaguer (he's 4½ inches high), #1306 P-7436; or a Baseball Topper Set (an umpire, catcher and player), #2113 P-2473.

CHECKLIST

1. Send out invitations
2. Buy or borrow a wood-burning kit
3. Buy baseball cards
4. Buy baseball hats
5. Get Baseball Trivia Game
6. Order baseball figures for cake

3 | STAGE THREE

1. Buy one wooden baseball bat per child and, if you have a wood-burning kit, write each child's name on each bat.

2. Gather baseball posters from any teams and any other baseball paraphernalia to use as decoration. If your friends have any hats or banners, borrow them to hang around the party room. Save sports pages from the newspapers to use as a tablecloth.

3. If you have a color scheme that matches your child's favorite baseball team, make these colors the theme of the party. Buy paper plates, cups, balloons, streamers, banners and the like in these colors. You may also want to contact the team's office to get any "regulation" accessories they have on hand.

4. Buy tubes of colored frosting that match your team colors.

CHECKLIST

1. Get the wooden baseball bats
2. Collect baseball posters, hats, banners and sports pages from newspaper
3. Get table accessories
4. Buy tubes of cake frosting

4 | STAGE FOUR

1. Buy hot dogs, corn on the cob, peanuts (shelled), popcorn and sandwich bags for the popcorn (you may be able to find the red and white bags), and soft drinks.

2. Bake the Baseball Diamond Cake.

3. Decorate the house with all the baseball paraphernalia you have collected. Set the table.

4. Make a Happy Birthday banner in your chosen colors.

5. Collect the baseball caps to give out as each child arrives.

CHECKLIST

1. Buy food
2. Bake cake
3. Decorate house and set table
4. Make banner
5. Prepare baseball caps

ACTIVITIES

1. Trivia Baseball • This is our version of baseball for ages eight to twelve; it can be played in your party room or even in your backyard, if you're lucky enough to have one. You'll need to set up bases in your party room or backyard and to choose some trivia questions that are appropriate to the age of your guests. The questions can be baseball-related or just sports-related.

Divide the guests into teams (they can vote on their team name, you can name them after your hometown professional or high school teams, or your child's favorite teams). Now make your birthday child "Team Manager"; he can be "in charge" of everything, including having referee privileges (we have to take some liberties here!). Play a variation of real baseball: Have the manager choose one team to be "at bat" and the other team to "man the bases." Then the first baseman asks the batter a trivia question. If he answers correctly, he can advance to first base and the next person goes "up to bat." If not, he gets two more chances, and each wrong answer counts as a "strike." Three strikes and you're out! Then the next team member is up to bat. Three "outs" and the teams switch places. Thus the first team will now be asking the questions and the other team will be answering. You can keep this going with a time limit or a score limit (i.e., the first person to get three home runs wins the game).

2. Baseball Bingo • This game is appropriate for all ages. Distribute one of the baseball bingo cards that you made to each guest. You can appoint the birthday boy "reader"—he gets to read the cards to the other kids. Remember, make sure that you have a matching baseball card for each player you have on the bingo cards. (This is easier than it sounds. If you buy several extra baseball card packages, you will get duplicates of the baseball cards you used to make the bingo cards.) Now you play the game just as you would regular bingo—play it to "cover"—that means, the winner has to have covered all the baseball figures on his card.

3. Trading Cards • If this group of kids collects cards, give out extra baseball card packages and let them trade the cards to their hearts' content. You may be surprised at how much fun they'll have just chatting away about who has which card.

4. Spoonball Race • This is also appropriate for all ages. Divide the guests into two teams. Give each person a soup spoon (preferably one with a plastic handle) and a lightweight baseball (you can use a small Wiffle ball). To start the race, designate starting and finishing lines. Have one member of each team stick the handle of the spoon in his mouth, place a ball on the spoon and walk to the finish line and back. Now he has to put the baseball in the next teammate's spoon (with his hands). You get the idea. The first team to finish the race wins.

5. LUNCH

M • E • N • U

Hot Dogs
Corn on the Cob
Peanuts
Popcorn
Baseball Diamond Cake
Soft Drinks and/or Punch

TIP

If, at your Baseball party, you're going to play a real baseball game in the backyard or at the park, have batting and ball-catching practice as the guests arrive. Maryann Pope did; she also had a beanbag toss and several toy vehicles on hand for anyone who didn't want to play ball.

72

See the recipes on page 220.

ENTERTAINMENT

The activities will take up plenty of time at this party. But if you want additional entertainment, you can screen the movie *The Bad News Bears*. You can also invite a local high school baseball player or coach to talk to the boys about the "inside" sport of baseball.

If you have a backyard and want the children to actually play a baseball game, go ahead and do so. You then probably won't have the time to play all the games listed. You can choose any of them for a change of pace after the baseball game. All of them will be terrific complements to the game.

FAVORS

The baseball bats with each child's name on them will be a huge hit! And remember, the kids are also taking home their baseball hats. You can give the popular Matt Christopher sports books as favors for ages six and up. These favors are truly the final touch to a party your son and his friends will remember for some time!

Forgive us for a note here about our supposition that only boys will enjoy this party. As you already know by our philosophy, anything you want goes. If your daughter just loves baseball and this is the party of her dreams, give it for her! If your son wants to invite girls to this party, by all means do so! They will have as much fun as the boys, and you'll find all the games as appropriate for girls as for boys.

For additional favors, you can buy baseballs or softballs and have the kids sign them, so that each child ends up with a ball autographed by all the guests at the party.

* If your child is a collector, give him something for his collection at every birthday. John Rubin started collecting maps when he was very young, and by the time he was a teenager, he had a valuable collection from his parents. You can add to or build your child's collection of coins, photographs, antique toys, etc.

BIKE-A-THON

Ages 6 and up

If your child and her bike are inseparable, have we got a party for her! Whether she is four or ten, having a party at which everyone gets to decorate their bikes and then participate in a one-of-a-kind bike parade will result in a birthday to remember.

1 STAGE ONE

1. The activities at this party—decorating the bikes and having a bike parade—may take more than our usual two hours. Starting in the late morning and ending in the early afternoon should give everyone enough time to have a ball. And, if you remember to get extra help, you won't be overwhelmed.

2. Make your guest list and invitations.

INVITATION

The illustration of a bicycle (below) can be xeroxed and then individually colored in by the birthday child.

CHECKLIST

1. Plan time for party
2. Make guest list and invitations

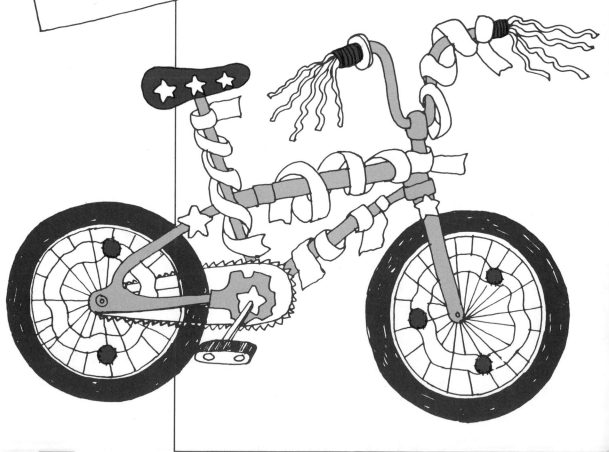

STAGE TWO

1. Call RSVPs. Remind them to bring their bikes. Children four to six can bring tricycles; older kids can bring two-wheelers. If there is a guest who doesn't have a bike, arrange to borrow one.

2. Gather the things the children will need to decorate the bikes. These include rolls of crepe paper in different colors, tissue paper, ribbons, glue, several scissors, twist ties, clothespins, playing cards, plastic toys and/or charms, tin cans, strips of Mylar, bottle caps and any other decorating accessories you can find. Have cardboard and magic markers for making signs and a birthday banner.

3. Set the menu. Buy the basic ingredients. If you want to make any substitutions, plan them now.

4. Prepare the prizes and favors. Visit your local sports or discount store and you may be surprised at the number, variety and reasonable prices of bicycle accessories. Possible prizes and favors include bike horns, pom pom streamers for handlebars, odometers, baskets, mirrors, reflectors, racing grips, and headlights. Prices range from $1.29 to $5.99 per item.

CHECKLIST

1. Call RSVPs
2. Collect decorations
3. Decide on the menu
4. Get prizes and favors

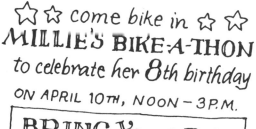

☆ ☆ come bike in ☆ ☆
MILLIE'S BIKE-A-THON
to celebrate her 8th birthday
ON APRIL 10TH, NOON – 3 P.M.

BRING YOUR BIKE

222 IRVING PLACE R.S.V.P 555-2345

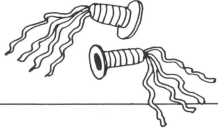

3 STAGE THREE

CHECKLIST

1. Prepare food
2. Prepare for picnic
3. Get favors ready
4. Collect extra bikes
5. Prepare prizes
6. Prepare camera and film

1. Prepare the food. You can bake and decorate the cake today. Make the fried chicken and refrigerate. Buy any other ingredients you need. Remember, this is a picnic so get drinks you can carry. Chips are best in individual bags.

2. There is no need to decorate the house or set a table. Lunch is a picnic, either at the local park or in your backyard. You will also have to gather any picnic accessories—blankets, plastic forks and spoons, thermoses, etc.

3. Get the favors ready and wrap them. Mark the prizes to differentiate them from the favors.

4. Borrow any extra bikes you need today so you have one less thing to do tomorrow morning.

5. Prepare a list of prizes you will be giving out. Decide on the categories with your child. Give a prize to everyone.

6. Prepare the camera and have lots of extra film. Assign the photography to one of your helpers so you won't have to remember to take pictures.

ACTIVITIES

1. Decorating the Bikes • Have the bike decorations in plastic bowls so the children can start decorating the bikes as they arrive. It will take them some time to decorate their bikes. Take pictures, as the kids are having a great time! Encourage themes and give a few suggestions to get them started—western, punk, space, etc.

2. Prizes • Give out prizes for the bikes. Possible categories include most unusual, most beautiful, most colorful, best use of a certain color, best theme, most outrageous, funniest, bike most like its owner.

3. Bike Parade • If you are having the picnic at the park, have a parade of the bikes to the park. If your picnic is in the backyard, organize a parade around your neighborhood. Make sure you have enough supervision.

TIP

Don't overlook the use of home computers, instant print shops and copy machines that print in color, enlarge or shrink images for creating unusual and personal invitations.

4. Breaking Away • Chances are you won't have enough time to show a movie, but if you should need to, you can show it after the picnic lunch. This is really a contingency plan, just in case it should start raining in the middle of your parade.

5. PICNIC

M • E • N • U

Racer's Fried Chicken
Chips
Fresh Fruit
Lemonade
Spoke Cake

See the recipes on pages 220–22.

FAVORS

The favors are the decorated bikes and the bike accessories. You can also buy *BMX* magazines.

MILLIE
NEW HAMPSHIRE

Nora Ephron's rule: Keep the favors simple. It is embarrassing to come home with a favor that cost more than the gift!

80

CHEERLEADING PARTY

Ages 8–13

 G reat high school cheers from our past, right? Well, maybe, but at this moment they are even being taught by Louise Vaughan to six- and seven-year-olds at The Center for Early Education in Los Angeles. It's not that the Center has school sports teams; it doesn't. But the little girls love cheerleading, so an after-school course was set up and it is oversubscribed every semester.

 You can't be too old or too young to love the spirit, the fun and the excitement that cheerleading provides for many young girls. For them, the Cheerleading party is a real delight.

1 STAGE ONE

1. Do some research to find a couple of teenage cheerleaders from your local high school. Hire them to come and teach the girls their cheers and routines.

2. Find out the color and/or kind of outfit these cheerleaders wear. You can ask the girls to wear tights and leotards, pants and sweaters, or shorts and shirts in those colors. Make it clear that they don't have to buy any costumes.

3. Make and send the invitations.

INVITATION

The invitation is an illustration of a megaphone. Make one copy of our illustration and fill out the information on the paper megaphone. Now xerox as many invitations as you need on colored paper matching your cheerleading colors and cut out the shape of the megaphone. Send in envelopes that are also in the cheerleading colors. Write "Cheers" on the outside.

CHECKLIST

1. Find cheerleaders
2. Decide on costumes
3. Make and send invitations

HIP HIP HOORAY! IT'S ANDREA'S
☆ ☆ ☆ ☆ ∙ ☆ BIRTHDAY
FRIDAY APRIL 10 at 555 WIGWAM WAY
fun begins at 7:00 p.m. pickup at 9:00
please say YES: 555-5555
☆ bring blue pants
and yellow top
to cheer in!
☆

cheers
Jane Jones
Riverway
Conn. 06877

STAGE TWO

1. Call RSVPs. Remind everyone about the cheerleading costumes and colors.

2. At any large discount or toy store, buy pom-poms and megaphones for all the girls (you can find them sold in sets). You may want to get extras to use as centerpieces for the table.

3. Start planning the activities.

- The "professional" cheerleaders will take some time to teach the girls a full routine. Ask them about music, and get the appropriate records or tapes. When the girls are ready to perform, make sure you have an audience.
- In addition to the cheerleading, you can set up some play make-up and temporary mousse hair colors for the girls to play with. Get these now.
- With your child, make up questions for the Schooly-Wed-Game (you need only one copy for the "moderator," who can be the birthday child or a parent).
- Pop lots of popcorn for the Popcorn Relay.
- The girls will help to make dinner.

4. This is a party that should, if at all possible, be videotaped and shown to the girls that night. If you don't own a camera, you can rent one for the day at most video stores. The girls will delight in seeing how their hard work—learning the cheerleading routines—paid off. Take snapshots as well. You can give each girl a picture of herself in costume doing cheerleading configurations. They will all treasure this shot!

5. You will need a fairly empty party room so the girls will have enough space to learn and practice their routines. If you don't have a basement, recreation room or playroom, push aside the furniture in a room they can use. It is worth the trouble!

6. Go over the menu. It is a simple one, and the girls can participate in making the dinner. Get the makings and toppings this week.

7. Start thinking about the favors. Records or tapes are big hits, as are school banners or pennants. Buy them now, especially if you have to order unusual favorites.

CHECKLIST

1. Call RSVPs; check on costumes
2. Get cheerleading accessories
3. Plan activities
4. Arrange for video equipment
5. Arrange for an appropriate party room
6. Go over menu
7. Prepare favors
8. For a slumber party, make additional plans now

Ann Hollister's favorite slumber party trick is to have the girls dip their socks or T-shirts in water and place them in the freezer. In the morning, you have "Sock Sculptures"—the clothes have frozen into funny shapes!

* Jessica Yellin's favorite party was a "Miss America Pageant" where the girls dressed up in their best and had to come prepared with a performance routine. Each contestant was a winner because there were as many categories as guests.

8. This party can easily become a slumber party by adding a few alternatives:

- Be sure to ask the girls to bring their own sleeping bags.
- Buy Trivial Pursuit, Ad Libs and Body Boggle at any toy store. Make up a scrambled word game that relates to cheerleading.
- A slumber party is a great time to show a movie. Dressed in pajamas, with popcorn in their hands, the girls will be in the perfect mood to watch a film, especially a comedy which will make them giggle and laugh together (like *Romancing the Stone* or *Pretty in Pink*).
- Add other dishes to your menu (nachos and popcorn for snacks; bagels, cinnamon and hot chocolate for breakfast).

3 | STAGE THREE

1. Buy the ingredients for the Wacky Cake, tacos, and ice cream sundaes, and sodas or juices. (You will also need nachos, popcorn and the makings for the breakfast of your choice if this is a slumber party.)

2. The favors will be the pom-poms and megaphones. If you bought records or tapes, gather them together and have them ready for tomorrow.

3. You can set the table today or do it the morning of the party. Repeat the cheerleading colors in the table decor. Make it easier on yourself by using paper plates, cups, etc. You can put extra pom-poms on the table for decoration.

4. Prepare everything you will need for the games. Remember pencil and paper for the Schooly-Wed-Game.

ACTIVITIES

1. Cheerleading • This can take up at least one or two hours. The girls will learn the cheers and routines, and then want to perform them. Try to be available to watch the finished routines—it's a lot more fun with an audience! Again, try to videotape the routines. Be prepared to watch a lot of reruns!

C H E C K L I S T

1. Buy ingredients for food
2. Get favors ready
3. Set and decorate the table
4. Prepare all games

TIP

Older children love mysteries. You can buy *Two Minute Mysteries*, published by Scholastic Magazine, and help the kids play these popular games.

2. The Schooly-Wed-Game • Divide the girls into "couples." Then have the moderator ask all the couples the same question ("Who will she say is her favorite teacher?," "What television program does she love?" etc.). One member of each couple writes down her answer and the other guesses that answer. For each correct answer, a couple wins five points. The couple with the highest score wins.

3. DINNER • The girls will help you make dinner.

M • E • N • U

Tacos
Ice Cream Sundaes
and Toppings
Wacky Cake
Soda or Juices

See the recipes on pages 222–23.

4. Popcorn Relay • You'll need one large bowl of popcorn, two empty bowls and two wooden mixing spoons. Divide the girls into two teams. At the sound of "Go," a member of each team runs to the popcorn, scoops up a spoonful and races back to empty the spoon into her team's bowl. The next team member then does the same thing. The first team to empty one bowl and fill the other wins. This is more difficult than you think—popcorn is lightweight and subject to being blown off the spoon.

5. Body Boggle • Also known as Twister, this game can be bought at any toy store. The object is to put your hands and legs on different colored dots and, by following the instructions, manage to get your body all tangled up. It is a lot of fun and kids love it.

6. Trivial Pursuit • Divide the children into teams and play any version they like.

FAVORS

The favors are megaphones, pom-poms and/or any other appropriate items, such as school banners and pennants.

✳ Jessica Leader, a sixth grader at the Brearley School in New York, invited her classmates to play her invention, "The Schooly-Wed-Game," which was an adaptation of a television game show. It got such "high ratings" that other game shows began to be the hit of the birthday party circuit. Jessica encouraged the girls to watch the show before the party to see how the game is played.

CHEFS
IN THE
KITCHEN

Ages 5–12

Y ou may not want to wait for a birthday to give this party! Most kids are fascinated by the kitchen, and will really respond to making their own pizza rather than having it served in a pizza parlor. Making homemade ice cream will make eating it ten times more fun. When they form a pretzel with their own hands, dip it in salt and watch it crisp into the same pretzel they get in the pretzel bag, they'll be ecstatic. All the mystery of how ingredients turn into the food they recognize and love will disappear—and they will marvel at their own abilities and ingenuity. Their favorite foods will never be the same again!

An added, perhaps obvious, thought: This party is chock full of activities that need the space a large kitchen provides. If you have a galley kitchen or an otherwise small kitchen, limit this party to just a few children.

1 STAGE ONE

CHECKLIST

1. Discuss party theme
2. Plan invitation
3. Buy chef's aprons
4. Arrange for help

1. Spend some time discussing a cooking party with your child. Talk about his favorite foods and how you can make them. Our menu includes making pizza, pretzels and ice cream and, if you have the time, decorating cupcakes. Your child may come up with something else he would like to make. Why not try to find that recipe, adapt it for the group and put it on the menu.

2. Start planning the invitation. You can send it at this time or wait to do so a month before the party.

INVITATION

Buy one wooden mixing spoon per child at any supermarket. Write the child's name on the outer end of the handle with a permanent marking pen (see illustration). Now write:

COME TO AMANDA'S CHEFS IN THE KITCHEN PARTY

On the other side of the spoon, write:

DATE: TIME: PLACE: RSVP

(You can ask your guests to bring their wooden spoons with them to the party.)

Send the spoon in a padded envelope. If you have scratch and sniff food stickers, put them on the outside of the envelope.

3. Buy white chef's kitchen aprons for every guest (including the adults who will be helping you). Buy toques—chef's hats—for each as well. You can usually find these items at kitchen supply stores. Gather permanent markers in different colors and store with the aprons and toques. Once you have your RSVP list, personalize each apron and toque for your guests.

4. Invite some adults or teenagers to assist you. (Some teenagers love to cook and would be terrific helpers. Make sure that any teen you hire does have some kitchen experience. As always, meet with the helpers ahead of time so you can fully detail what you expect from them. Chances are, if you are clear about this "job" description, you will be satisfied with the results.) You'll always be grateful for help at any of these parties, and this one, especially, needs the assistance of other "grown-ups." There will be several cooking activities going on at the same time, and you can't be everywhere at once. The addition of adult supervision will make this party run smoothly and safely.

STAGE TWO 2

1. There is not much else to do this far ahead of time because the items you will need for this party—namely, food—need to be bought just before the party.

CHECKLIST

1. Send invitation

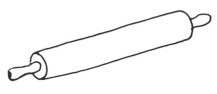

STAGE THREE 3

1. Call your RSVPs and make up your final guest list. Include those adults and/or teenagers you have asked to come to help.

2. Now that you have your guest list, if you'd like, you can paint the guests' names on the chef aprons and toques. Set them aside until the day of the party so they won't get dirty.

3. The kitchen already has "atmosphere." The mood is set just by the kitchen, the aprons and toques. If this is a birthday party, you may want to hang a birthday banner up high in the kitchen. You can buy paper plates and cups with designs of

CHECKLIST

1. Call RSVPs
2. Paint names on aprons and toques
3. Get plates and cups
4. Plan menu and type recipes
5. Buy film
6. Gather utensils

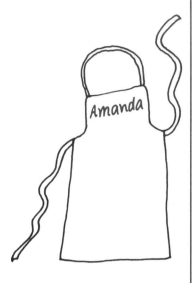

Amanda

food (these are not always stocked in party stores, but can be bought in supermarkets, where they are sold for general home and picnic use).

4. Make the final decision about the menu. Type each recipe out on a separate sheet and duplicate. If your child is old enough to do this, assign this task to him.

5. Buy a lot of film. You will want a group shot and individual shots of each guest "in uniform" for the cover of that recipe book. Then you will want to take candid shots of the children as they are cooking.

6. Analyze your exact utensil needs and organize a day ahead. Borrow from a neighbor if you need more. Be sure to include in this list mixing spoons, frying pans, mixing bowls, cutting boards, pizza pans, cookie sheets, ice cream bowls and spoons. Keep in mind the number of guests and dishes you will be cooking. Have someone pick these up the day before the party.

4 | STAGE FOUR

1. If you are using our menu, here are the items you will need from your market:

milk	pizza toppings
whipping cream	(your choice or see our menu)
sugar	coarse salt
vanilla	rock salt
yeast	baking soda
unbleached flour	about eight baking potatoes
olive oil	

2. Be sure those extra kitchen tools are delivered to your house today.

3. You may want to make the pizza dough today. It takes about an hour and a half to rise and you may not want to wait during the party. So follow the instructions for making the dough in our pizza recipe. When it has risen, refrigerate it until the party day. (If you want to make it even easier, you can buy ready-made pizza dough at your market.) Some children may enjoy knowing how the dough is made, so it

CHECKLIST

1. Buy food
2. Check on tools
3. Make pizza dough
4. Bake cupcakes

could be part of the fun to have the ingredients ready to make your own dough.

4. Bake cupcakes. If this is a birthday party, use the cupcakes as birthday cakes. On the party day the children will decorate the cupcakes with powdered sugar frosting, sprinkles and silver balls. You can then add the candles on the birthday child's cupcake. (Or, for a fun variation, put one candle on each cupcake so everyone can blow them out together.) On the other hand, you may want to take the time and let the children write their own names on the cupcakes during the party. Frosting tubes are available in the supermarket. Either way, cupcakes are a nice change from a cake.

Serve them with your homemade ice cream.

STAGE FIVE | **5**

1. Lay out all the tools you will need. Gather the food in one place. Let the children do all the measuring.

CHECKLIST

1. Arrange food and tools

ACTIVITIES

As the children arrive, give them each a personalized apron and toque. Since all the children will probably not be arriving together, you will want to give the prompt arrivals something to do. Direct them to a table where you have lots of old food magazines, several pairs of scissors, glue and sheets of cardboard which will be the covers for their recipe books. Let them start making their collages. Have copies of the recipes ready. Throughout the party they can return to this activity (whenever they are not involved in the cooking) to complete their collage.

Now gather everyone in the kitchen. Organize the activities so that each child has a chance to cook at least a part of each dish. The easiest way to do this is to make one dish at a time. You can do this most efficiently with a small group. If you have more children, have some make the pizza while the others make the ice cream. If you prefer, you can ask the children to decide who wants to cook what and cook the dishes

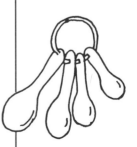

simultaneously (the pizza needs the ovens, but the ice cream only needs the kitchen or dining room or porch floor) so the kids won't be getting in each other's way.

Here's the way Amanda Gordon, our eight-year-old friend from Santa Barbara, did it for her birthday. She invited twelve children to her party, so her mother Ronna divided the children into four groups, each headed by an adult chief cook. The first group cut up the pizza toppings while the second group began to make the pretzel dough. The third group began making the ice cream, and the fourth decorated their own cupcakes. Then they switched: The second group rolled the ice cream while the first topped a pizza. The third decorated their cupcakes and the fourth formed some pretzels. They then switched again—you get the idea. Just remember, be flexible so that everyone can have a chance to try a little of everything. The point is to have the children learn how food is prepared and to have them feel that they prepared it. And with adult help, it will go as smoothly as possible.

FAVORS

Each child leaves this party with a personalized apron and toque, and his very own recipe book with his own creative collage on the cover, a huge smile on his face and stories to tell for a long time. Don't be surprised to get a call from the children's mothers, who will be full of awe at their children's newly found interest in what goes on in the kitchen.

By the way, Amanda Gordon has already been asked by her friends to book the Gordon kitchen again for her ninth birthday.

Amanda Gordon's mom Ronna put leftovers in lunch bags wrapped in ribbons and sent them home to the parents as evidence of the kids' cooking prowess.

M • E • N • U

Potato Chips
Pizza
Pretzels
Ice Cream
Chocolate Cupcakes

The ages and number of your guests will probably determine whether you tackle one, two or five recipes.

POTATO CHIPS

**8 baking potatoes, peeled
pinch of salt**

Preheat the oven to 400 degrees.

Slice the potatoes very finely in a food processor. Put them in water to prevent browning. As you are making some of the other dishes, you can have a couple of children place the potato slices in one layer on a well-greased cookie sheet. Bake them in the oven until they are lightly brown. Remove with tongs, turn over, and bake until other side is lightly brown. Put the ready chips in a basket until they are all done and you are ready to serve.

PIZZA

Making the Dough (you can do this the day before):

Makes two 9-inch pizzas

  1 envelope active dry yeast
  1 tablespoon sugar
1½ cups warm water
**3¼ cups unbleached bread
    flour or all-purpose flour**
  ½ teaspoon salt
  ¼ cup olive oil

In a mixing bowl, combine the yeast and sugar. Add the water and stir. Set a timer for 5 minutes. When it rings, the yeast will be bubbling (if it isn't, start again with a new package of yeast).

Put 3 cups of flour in a large mixing bowl. Add the salt. Place a soup ladle in the middle to form

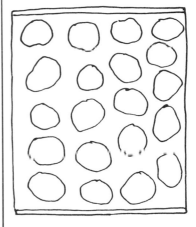

✱ The Happy Birthday message doesn't have to be confined to the birthday cake. For years Calvin and Alice Trillin's daughters have had the honor of receiving a pizza with the words "Happy Birthday" spelled out in veggies. The donor is a family friend, Larry Goldberg, who owns Goldberg's Pizzeria in New York.

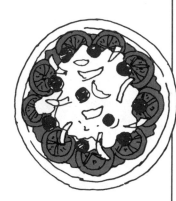

a well and remove. Pour that yeast mixture into this well and add the oil. Slowly mix everything in the bowl. When the dough is soft but together, put it on a floured cutting board.

Knead the dough with your hands. (Children love this part! Let them each have a turn at kneading the dough, but know that it will stick to their fingers and you will have to wash them immediately! If you made this the day before, have them "pretend" knead the dough when you have removed it from the refrigerator. It won't hurt the dough and they'll love it!) If the dough is too sticky, add the remaining ¼ cup flour. Keep kneading. This will take about 15 minutes—enough time to have each child knead it and feel that he really worked!

When done, make a ball out of the dough. Oil a large bowl and put the dough into it. Turn it over a couple of times to make sure it is oiled on all sides. Cover the bowl with plastic wrap, set it in a warm place (an oven that is not lit is fine) and let it rise for about 1½ hours. Flatten it; now place it into another bowl and refrigerate for 20 minutes to 1 hour. (If you are making it the night before, leave it in the refrigerator until the next day.)

In the morning, divide the dough into two halves. Each half will make one pizza.

Making the Pizza:

Suggested Toppings:

Tomato slices
Fresh chopped basil
Sliced mushrooms
Sliced salami and/or pepperoni
Sliced green peppers
Cheeses (mozzarella,
**   Parmesan, Cheddar)**

Preheat the oven to 500 degrees.

Place some large tiles in the oven. This will make the pizza crust cook more evenly when you place the pans on them.

Flour a cutting board. Take out one ball of dough at a time and flatten with a rolling pin. (You really can't flatten it too much, so let each child have a chance to roll the dough. If it does get too thin, you can make it into a ball and start rolling again.) Put the dough on a pizza pan. Brush the top with olive oil until it is really wet with it.

Now top the pizza with the toppings you have chosen. Start with the cheese or cheeses and then arrange any or all of the others. Top with drops of more olive oil and place the pizza in the oven. Bake for only about 8 to 10 minutes, or until the bottom and sides of the crust are lightly brown.

Note: Because it doesn't take very long to make this pizza, you can have one group make one and then another group make another. If you are having twelve children, as Amanda did, try making four pizzas. They'll eat them, and even if they don't, there will likely be some hungry helpers who will!

PRETZELS

Makes about 15 pretzels

margarine for greasing
 ½ cup kosher salt
 2 tablespoons boiling water
 1 envelope (¼ ounce) active
    dry yeast
 ¾ cup hot water
 2 tablespoons brown sugar
2½ cups flour
 10 cups water
 10 tablespoons baking soda

Preheat the oven to 475 degrees.

Grease two cookie sheets and sprinkle them with kosher salt.

In a large bowl, mix the yeast with 2 tablespoons boiling water until the yeast dissolves. Add ¾ cup hot water and the brown sugar, and mix with a wooden spoon. Now have the children take turns adding the flour, 1 tablespoon at a time, while you keep stirring to get a smooth dough.

Have the kids wash their hands while you put the dough on a floured cutting board. Now let each child take a turn kneading the dough. Set a timer for 5 minutes and have the children keep kneading. When it goes off, pull off pieces of dough about 1½ inch round and roll out into little snakes about 12 inches long. Twist one pretzel as per illustration and then let the kids shape them.

While the children are kneading the dough, have another child and an adult prepare two large frying pans, each filled with 5 cups water and 5 tablespoons baking soda. (Having two pans will speed up the cooking process. But you can get by with one.) Bring both to a boil.

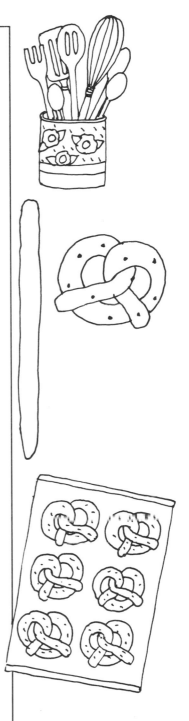

Take each shaped pretzel and place on a spatula. Dip the spatula into the boiling water and count to thirty. (Kids love to count, so have them count as you hold the pretzel in the water. If the kids are eleven or twelve years old, they can handle the spatula in the water.) When you reach thirty, the pretzel is done. Remove it from the water and slide it onto the salted cookie sheet. (If it doesn't slide off too easily, help it with a knife.) When all the pretzels are on the cookie sheets, have the kids sprinkle them with more salt.

Bake the pretzels for 6 to 8 minutes. Watch them! When they are evenly brown they're ready. Don't let them burn! If you find that some are getting brown and others aren't, just turn the cookie sheet around (it probably means that the heat in your oven is uneven). When they have cooled slightly, they are ready to be eaten.

Note: It is hard for children to cook and not to eat. They have to wait for the pizza and ice cream, but the pretzels and the chips can be eaten as soon as they are cool. As a matter of fact, they are best then—nice and chewy. So why not let them eat the pretzels as they are ready and while they are still working hard on the other foods!

ICE CREAM

This ice cream is a lot of fun to make, but you should know that it doesn't get as hard as store-bought ice cream. So advertise it to your children as "soft" ice cream. We first heard about this ice cream when Jackie Olney, the

Los Angeles cook who has a radio show, answered a caller's question about making ice cream quickly. We couldn't believe our ears! It didn't seem possible that rolling a coffee can on a hard floor makes ice cream! But it does, and if you think we were surprised, wait until you see the faces of your children!

Serves 4

crushed ice (large pieces)
¾ cup rock salt
1 cup milk
1 cup whipping cream
½ cup sugar
½ teaspoon vanilla extract
Ice cream toppings (optional)

Put the milk, whipping cream, sugar and vanilla in a 1-pound coffee can. Close the lid tightly. Put the entire can into a 5-pound coffee can. Pack the section around the smaller can with crushed ice and rock salt (you may want to wear rubber gloves because your hands get cold handling the ice). Close the can tightly.

Now roll the can back and forth on a hard floor, between two pairs of children about 4 feet apart, for 10 minutes (and again for another 10 minutes). Have each set of children roll it back and forth for about 4 minutes (you can set another timer) so they won't get bored and all the children will get a chance to roll the can. To double the yield, you can have two cans going at the same time and keep eight children busy. At Amanda's party, one group rolled

the can while another group was finishing the pretzels.

After 10 minutes, open the outer can and throw out the rock salt and what will be melted ice. Open the inner can and mix everything together (be sure to scrape the sides of the can). Replace the lid and again pack the ice and another ¾ cup of rock salt. Roll again for 10 minutes. When done, the ice cream will be quite soft. Let the children have a taste, then put it in the freezer until you are ready to serve the cupcakes and ice cream.

CHOCOLATE CUPCAKES

Making cupcakes is certainly a fun and manageable little chef's activity. There are a number of possibilities here. (1) The children can mix the batter together; (2) you mix the batter before the party and the children fill the cupcake tins and bake them; or (3) you bake the cupcakes before the party and allow the children to decorate them.

Makes 12–14 cupcakes

  2 cups sugar
  2 cups flour
  4 tablespoons cocoa
  ½ cup butter, melted
  ½ cup milk
  ½ tablespoon vinegar
  2 eggs
  1 teaspoon baking soda
  1 teaspoon baking powder
  1 cup boiling water

Preheat the oven to 375 degrees.

In a bowl or in a food processor with the steel blade, mix together all the ingredients. The mixture will look very thin, but don't worry.

Grease a 9-cup muffin pan and fill each cup with the batter ¾ full. Bake for 20 minutes.

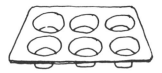

CHOCOLATE FROSTING

Makes frosting for 15 cupcakes

  2 squares baking chocolate
  2 cups powdered sugar
  ½ stick (¼ cup) butter
2-3 tablespoons Decaf
       morning coffee
Collection of sprinkles, red
  hearts, silver balls

Mix the chocolate, sugar and butter together in a bowl. Add just enough coffee to make the mixture smooth.

Have each child dip his cupcake into the frosting. Let set, then decorate.

Older children will have fun using ready-made icing in tubes. Also have on hand colored sprinkles, red hearts, silver balls, etc., to decorate to their heart's delight. Have the candles ready as well, either for the birthday child or one for everyone's cupcakes.

Use paper muffin liners to insure that the cupcakes come out easily.

97

DINER PARTY

Ages 8–12

W e're not really sure why, but many children are fascinated with the 1950's. Some of them seem to be more excited about that era than those of us who lived it! Whether it's the poodle skirts or duck tail or bob-bob-a-doo beat of the music, something is spellbinding our 80's kids back to the 50's world. If your child is one of these devotees, he may be thrilled with this party.

1 STAGE ONE

1. Make your guest list.
2. Make and send the invitations.

INVITATION

This invitation is a menu you can xerox. Write text on the other side of the invitation:

CHECKLIST

1. Make guest list
2. Make and send invitations
3. Discuss the 50's with your child
4. Collect items for Diner
5. Prepare decorations; make signs

SPECIAL OF THE DAY!

come have
DINNER AT THE
DINER
Food Plus Fun!
DRESS 50's!
Saturday, Feb. 4th
>> 5-7 PM <<
5555 Morning Drive
RSVP. 555-1234

3. Discuss the 50's with your child, sharing your memories (and perhaps your pictures) with her. The next time you're in a diner together, take notice of the signs, decor, posters, menu items, etc., so you can adapt it all and use it for your party.

4. Start collecting items you will need. Buy fake money at your local toy store. Collect or borrow posters from the 50's. Get a cash register (a toy one is perfect—or you can use a calculator/adding machine and a cigar box for the "cash drawer"), records from that era and tagboard or cardboard to

make signs. At the stationery store, buy pads of "Guest Checks" for the waitresses to take dinner orders and buy tickets for the patrons.

5. Make a list of decorations you will need:

- a counter (you can make one with a long table or an ironing board)
- card tables with red checkered tablecloths (plastic or paper) and enough chairs for everyone on your guest list
- signs to hang around the Diner: No Tipping—You Paid Enough!; OPEN; Air Conditioning; Worst Food in Town; Watch Your Money—Our Dog Is a Known Pickpocket; Slowest Service in Town; Cash Only—Your Credit Is No Good Here!; No Littering—You Drop It, You Clean It!; Self-Service—or You'll Never Eat!! (You'll probably come up with even more.)

STAGE TWO 2

1. Call the RSVPs.

2. If you need to buy, borrow or make any other decorations, arrange for them now.

3. Make a large poster as your food sign. Have your child decide on the outrageous prices.

4. Go over the list of games for this party.

CHECKLIST

1. Call RSVPs
2. Complete decorating plans
3. Make food poster
4. Prepare games

A sample sign:

JAY'S DINER

HOT DOG	$100
HAMBURGER	$150
PICKLES	$25
MUSTARD	$10
CATSUP	FREE
RELISH	$15
CHIPS	$50
COKE	$50
7-UP	$50
TOMATO	$10 extra
LETTUCE	$10 extra
CHEESE	$5 extra
ICE CREAM CONE	$100
FRIES	$75
CAKE	$100

SELF-SERVICE
OR
YOU'LL NEVER
EAT

3 STAGE THREE

1. Prepare all the food. Whatever you can't cook today (like the hamburgers) have ready to be cooked tomorrow. You can put the condiments in appropriate containers today. Leave as little as possible for tomorrow.

2. Put up all the decorations. Prepare the Diner room with the tables covered with the cloths, catsup bottles and paper napkins on each.

3. Prepare the uniforms for the adults and siblings who will be waiters and cashiers. Be sure the waiters and waitresses are dressed in 50's-like uniforms. Have white caps and aprons for everyone (or you can fold white kitchen towels into belts).

4. Assign someone the job of cashier and give him extra play money for change.

5. Prepare your help—teach them how to yell for food. If you know any "Diner" slang ("two pigs in a basket—hold the mayo"), teach it to the youngsters. They'll love it!

6. Make sure your stereo is working. You must have 50's music blaring at all times! Listening to the music from the movie *Grease* is great for Musical Chairs. If your children like to dance, make an area in the center between the tables for them to be able to boogie.

7. Prepare the favors. You can buy comic books and records or tapes almost anywhere. A cute gift for girls is socks with charms on them. You can buy or make these. You can also get ID bracelets at many toy stores.

ACTIVITIES

The main activity is ordering the food and eating it. It works this way: As the children arrive, greet them in the Diner and show them to their tables. Hand out a certain amount of the play money (say, $500) to each child. When all the children are seated, have them look at the large printed menu and order the food from the waiters. Have the waiters write the orders down on the "guest checks" and give each guest a ticket with a number on it. When their order is ready, the number will be called and they have to come and get their food (after they pay for it at the cashier).

CHECKLIST

1. Prepare food
2. Prepare the Diner's decorations
3. Get uniforms
4. Get cashier ready
5. Rehearse people who are helping
6. Get music ready
7. Prepare favors

Unusual ties for gift wrapping include twine, lace ribbons, hem binding, multicolored yarn tied together, raffia, fabric cut in strips and shoe laces.

You can serve all the foods you list on your menu at the Diner. If this is a birthday party and you want to have a cake, you can choose any one of the cakes in our parties (the Ugly Chocolate Cake from the Backwards party is a good choice, as are any of our cupcakes).

1. Telephone • Have them sit in a line and pass a word from ear to ear.

2. Hash House Dash • Divide the children into two teams. The trick is to have each child on each team walk across the Diner with a book on his head (set up some barriers so they have to walk around the tables and chairs). When a child gets across the room, he has to touch the next relay and pass the book. The first team to finish wins!

3. Scrambled Eggs • Play this in two teams. The kids have to unscramble the words relating to the Diner. (The suggestions here are best for children ten and older, but you can use much simpler words for younger ages.)

1. HOT DOG	THO OGD
2. JUKEBOX	KUEJXBO
3. PICKLE	KIELCP
4. CATSUP	SAPCTU
5. COKE	KOEC
6. MUSTARD	DURSAMT
7. MILK SHAKE	KIML HEKSA
8. STRAW	ARWTS
9. ICE CREAM	CIE RMACE
10. FRENCH FRIES	RHFCEN SERFI

4. Diner Hop • Play Musical Chairs using any rock-'n'-roll songs. You should have no trouble finding this music since so much of it has recently been reissued.

5. Grease • If your party is longer than two hours, you might want to screen the movie *Grease* for the children.

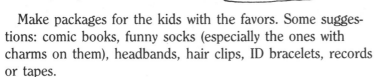

FAVORS

Make packages for the kids with the favors. Some suggestions: comic books, funny socks (especially the ones with charms on them), headbands, hair clips, ID bracelets, records or tapes.

✳ Jay Kriegel, who is now in his forties, had a Diner party for his tenth birthday. It was his favorite party, and was apparently memorable to others as well. Last year Jay ran into an old friend he had not seen for almost thirty years. The first thing his friend said was, "Remember that Diner party you had? It was the best party I ever went to!"

GHOST PARTY

Ages 5–10

W e adults normally equate ghosts with Halloween, but many children don't. Their love of ghosts is so intense that they would like nothing better than to have a Ghost party anytime. Witness Annie's son Marc, who at five years old begged for a Ghost birthday party (which in his version was a Ghostbusters party). It was a huge success, not only because the kids had such a wonderful time with all the games and decorations, but more, we believe, because it was held in March. The kids who usually waited with bated breath for Halloween so they could get dressed up as ghosts now had their chance to do so—and in the spring!

This party is so full of unusual games, and is so visually beautiful, that the children will be talking about it for weeks and will remember it for years.

1 STAGE ONE

1. Send out the ghost invitations and put together your RSVP list.

INVITATION

Buy one Tootsie Roll lollipop and one white handkerchief per guest. Place each handkerchief out on the table and write the invitation in a spiral around the edges (see illustration), making sure to leave the center white. When done, wrap the handkerchief around the lollipop, fasten with a ribbon or rubber band at the neck of the candy, dot two eyes with a black felt tip marker, and you have a little ghost invitation.

Send the invitation in a padded envelope. Marc's invitations were mailed with ghost stickers all over them.

2. Discuss the suggested menu with your child and ask for any added suggestions.

3. Start to shop for the following:
- black light (available at lighting and hardware stores; an incandescent bulb is about $3.75)
- colored light bulbs (blue is best)
- skeletons and skulls
- two flashlights
- gum ball machines with gum balls
- two dozen each light sticks and strings that light up in the dark, for decoration, waving around in the freeze dance and for favors
- ghost stickers for the envelopes for the invitations and for any decorations (if these are hard to find, draw or paint ghosts on the outside)

STAGE TWO

1. Call any guests who have not RSVP'd.

2. Call about the availability of pumpkins (if you are having this party at Halloween, try to find white pumpkins, available at some farms). If this party is being held in the spring, you can substitute honeydew melons for pumpkins.

3. Collect at least half a dozen white sheets.

4. Make your child's ghost costume. Just drape a twin sheet over the child, trim the bottom so he won't trip, and cut out eyes, nose, mouth and hands (it's easier to have the hands free to move around). If your child doesn't like anything on his head, make the same draped costume leaving the head free.

5. Buy:
   - colored balls of yarn (one color per guest), small plastic toys for the Spider Web and matching colored balloons
   - or gather the skeletons, skulls and any other "ghost" accessories you and your child have collected
   - toilet paper rolls (half as many as the number of guests)

6. Buy food items: green Jell-O; gingerman cookie cutter, cream cheese and raisins for the Ghost Sandwiches; sugar cubes, lemon extract and marshmallows for the Spook Cake.

CHECKLIST
1. Call RSVPs
2. Buy pumpkins or melons
3. Get sheets
4. Make ghost costume
5. Buy items for games
6. Buy food

107

3 STAGE THREE

CHECKLIST

1. Decorate room
2. Paint pumpkin or melons
3. Set table
4. Prepare food
5. Make Spider Web game

This is going to be fun! The party is so thematic that when everything falls into place you'll be as delighted as your child.

1. Start decorating the party room. Replace the bulbs with the blue ones. Hang white sheets everywhere you can (you can tape them with wrapping tape or staple them with an automatic staple gun at the place where the walls and ceilings join). Hang your black light in the room.

2. Paint black eyes on the green melons or pumpkins, or carve out eyes—no mouths or noses. Remember, these are ghosts! Place them around the house and a couple on the table.

3. Set the table. Cover with a white or black cloth. Place white paper plates on the black sheet, and black ones on the white sheet. We actually prefer using the white sheet with the black plates because the white Ghost Sandwiches look terrific on the black plates. Place a gum ball machine (full of candy or gum balls, depending on your philosophy about gum and the age of the children) at each place setting and cover with white cloth (you'll have to cut these out unless you can find handkerchiefs at the local five-and-dime that will cover the machines). You can also use white sandwich bags. Take a black marker and paint eyes on each shrouded machine so it looks as if a ghost is sitting at each plate.

4. Bake the cake and decorate with the eyes. Make the Slime Jell-O.

5. Make the Spider Web: Collect the colored balls of yarn. At each end tie a plastic toy. Hide the toy in a drawer, under a chair (it must be fastened to the chair), behind a door, etc. Now unwind the ball, slowly running the yarn in and around the objects in the room—up the dresser, around the chair, over and under the table, through a doorway and around a door— you get the idea. When you're done with a color, tie a balloon (in the same color) to the end of the yarn and let it hang. Repeat with all the yarns and plastic toys. Try to weave the yarns in and around the room so the striking effect is of a huge spider web in a room full of blue light and lined with sheets. It is spectacular—the children will never forget it! It

TIP

Ever run into a group of kids who wanted to know what the prizes were before they agreed to play the games? Janet Coberly from Atherton, California, did, at her son Peter's party. So she decided to award bottle caps as tokens that were redeemed at a "store" for prizes at the end of the party.

may sound like a lot of trouble to make but it really isn't. Get some adult to help and be sure to let your birthday child participate in this terrific activity.

ACTIVITIES

Set the mood as soon as you can. Place a cut-out of a ghost or hang an empty sheet with black eyes in the entryway or on the door. Be sure to take a picture of each ghost as it arrives at the party. If you hang balloons on the mailbox to alert your guests, use white ones with black "magic marker" eyes on them. If you have a tape or record player near the front door, or if you can make the sound reach the entrance, play a spooky song as everyone arrives (any Halloween themes, mystery movie themes, the *Ghostbusters* song, etc.). You get the idea—the mood was set a month ago when the ghost invitations arrived in the mail, and the atmosphere inside is super, but for that added touch, give them a little scary music as they step into this eerie wonderland you have created.

1. Spider Web • This game needs to be played first because it is already set up in the playroom and must be removed before you can do anything else. Have each child get hold of a balloon. If it is filled with helium, remove the balloon and let it float up to the ceiling. Let each child take the end of her yarn and start rolling it up into a ball, following the winding yarn until she gets to her little prize. You might want to give each child a 1- by 4-inch piece of cardboard around which she can rewind the yarn. When all the children are done, the spider web will have disappeared.

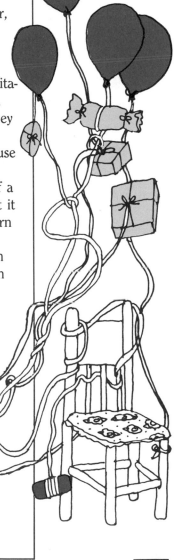

Nan Schwartz, from East Washington, New Hampshire, makes ghosts to hang on the trees in her front yard and throughout her house. For each ghost, she takes one pillow case, drops a rubber ball in it, ties it at the neck and turns it upside down. Then she threads a piece of yarn through the top and hangs it up.

2. Flashlight Tag • Darken the playroom and turn on the lamps with the blue lights in them. One person (it can be the birthday child to start) is "it." Give him the flashlight (have extra batteries around for emergencies!). All the other little ghosts hide. The "it" child has to find the other ghosts by shining the flashlight at them. As soon as a ghost is found he's "spooked" (or caught)! The last one to be found wins. Our friend Eric Schneider had Flashlight Tag parties (outdoors in springtime) for his eighth, ninth and tenth birthday parties. They must have been very successful to have been repeated again and again!

3. Mummy Wrap • Divide the guests into teams of two. Give each team a roll of toilet paper. On each team, one person wraps and the other is wrapped. The entire roll of toilet paper must be used! Whoever is done wrapping the mummy first, wins. For this game you can wrap the children in their ghost costume or you can have them remove it.

4. Freeze Dancing • This is a favorite for children of all ages. It is especially fun when they are dressed in costumes such as these ghosts. In your ghostly playroom, play appropriate music (the theme from the movie *Ghostbusters*, the *Flying Purple People Eater* or *Casper, the Friendly Ghost*). When the music stops, everyone freezes in their position. (This is a great time to take a picture of the children—they look so funny and silly! Be sure to use fast film as the room will be pretty dark.) If someone moves, she's out. The last person left wins.

5. Ghostly Masks • If you still have time, or if you prefer this activity to another, or if you need to quiet the children after some of this animated tumult, make masks. Gather some extra paper plates, markers, scissors, doilies, ribbons, feathers, lace, netting, false eyelashes and the like. Cut out holes for eyes, mouths and/or noses and have the children decorate the masks. When done they can wear them over their ghost costumes or take them home to hang in their rooms.

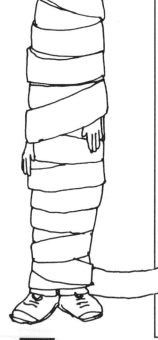

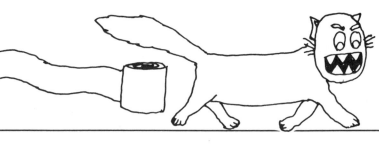

6. LUNCH

M • E • N • U

Ghost Sandwiches
Slime Jell-O
Spook Cake

See the recipes
on pages 223–24.

ENTERTAINMENT

Chances are you'll find you've scheduled too much, but our philosophy is that it is better to overplan. You can always drop an activity or simply move on if one isn't working the way you'd like.

FAVORS

The favors at this party are the gumball ghosts. If you need an alternative, you can give out light sticks, balls or strings by Lite Up or glow-in-the-dark shoelaces; paperback stories of ghosts; and, of course, photos of the kids in their costumes.

✳ It was also Janet Coberly and her kids who made a basic papier-mâché figure (he looked like a snowman) which is the birthday party mascot. He returns at each birthday party, dressed in the party theme. He has been a pirate, an astronaut, a cowboy and a fire fighter.

½ 🕯️🕯️ BIRTHDAY
DOUBLE YOUR FUN

Ages 4 and up

Annie's birthday is in August, Meredith's is on Christmas Day. Neither one of them ever had a real birthday party for school friends because they were always away on vacation.

We have the solution for all the Annies and Merediths whose birthday falls during vacations, and that's the Half Birthday. The idea is to plan the party on the child's half birthday (or thereabouts—the nice thing is that you can play around with the date for your convenience) and then build on the theme.

Our feeling is that a half birthday party can be even more fun than a regular birthday. First of all, your child will probably end up having two parties of some sort—one on the real birthday, when you are bound to have a small celebration, usually with the family. Second, our Half Birthday party is subtitled: "Double Your Fun!" And that's because we combine the theme of doing things both in halves and in doubles. This party is also the perfect theme for twins.

It is easy to get into the theme of this party, and easy, too, to get carried away with great ideas. Do just that—you can't be too outrageous at this party. And the more you plan along the half and double theme, the more your guests will delight in the idea, and the more delighted your previously birthday party–less child will feel.

1 STAGE ONE

CHECKLIST

1. Decide on party date
2. Prepare invitations

1. Plan the party for about the time that your child's half birthday will fall. Approximate the date for your added convenience.

2. Decide on the invitation. Plan to start and end the party on the half hour. For example, rather than the usual 1 p.m. to 3 p.m. party, make yours 12:30 to 2:30.

INVITATION

Buy wide, colored extra-long shoelaces—half as many pairs as there are guests. Have enough undecorated space on each so you can write on them. Arrange them on a table and write out the invitation on the shoelace.

PLEASE COME TO MEGHAN'S HALF BIRTHDAY/DOUBLE YOUR FUN PARTY Saturday, February 8th at 12:30-2:30pm

Each guest gets one shoelace (half a pair). The object here is to put together sets of twins. Each kid will call his twin (his telephone number is on the invitation) and they will come to the party dressed alike. Your job is to get the telephone numbers right!

Place each shoelace in an envelope. It is fun to decorate the envelope with stickers that you have cut in half (or double them up, if you like).

Another invitation is simpler and more obvious: Buy any invitations you like and cut them in half. Fill in half the information on one side and complete the data on the other. Again decorate the envelopes with halves or doubles of stickers.

please come to MEGHAN'S HALF BIRTHDAY: Double Your FUN PARTY

DATE____
TIME____
PLACE____
RSVP____

STAGE TWO

2

1. Sent out the invitations and make out the RSVP list.
2. Collect and/or buy the games and toys:
   - Bingo set (make it an inexpensive one—you will be cutting the cards in half)
   - pairs of toys (get as many as half the number of guests: 10 kids, 5 pairs of toys)
   - pairs of shoes and socks (get one pair of each for each guest: 10 kids, 10 pairs of shoes and 10 pairs of socks)
   - pads of paper and pencils (one per guest)
   - 1 Slinky
   - 1 set of Junior Trivia
   - 1 Body Boggle Game (Twister)
   - plenty of stickers (doubles of each)
3. Buy prizes for games—half-dollars are great; double small toys work, too.
4. Buy favors—double everything. The cost can add up so get small, inexpensive things that are age-appropriate. For younger children, get two each: LifeSaver rolls, pencils and erasers, key chains, puzzles, dice, playing cards, etc. For older kids, try comic books, hair clips, balls, puzzles, etc. Choose whatever you like; just remember to double the number so each child gets a twin of each favor.

CHECKLIST
1. Send invitation
2. Collect and buy items for games
3. Get prizes
4. Prepare favors

at 1244 Arbor Lane. RSVP at 553-4475 ☆ ☆ ☆ ☆ come dressed alike ☆ CALL 444-3546 For your twin with matching shoelace &

STAGE THREE

3

1. Either at this time or a week before the party, call anyone who has not responded.
2. Make arrangements for any extra help you may need. You can hire teenagers or ask adult members of your family or friends.
3. Go over the menu. Buy those items that are not easily and immediately available.
4. Buy paper plates, cups, napkins, a paper or plastic tablecloth, and plastic flatware. Buy extras for insurance. They have to be cut in half.

CHECKLIST
1. Call RSVPs
2. Get extra help
3. Go over menu
4. Buy decorations

4 STAGE FOUR

CHECKLIST

1. Buy food
2. Bake cake
3. Set table
4. Prepare toys
5. Prepare games
6. Prepare balloons and streamers

1. Buy pretzels, bread, peanut butter and tuna fish.

2. Bake the Half Birthday Cake.

3. Set the table: Cover with the paper or plastic tablecloth. Remember those stickers you bought? Your child will have fun decorating the tablecloth with them. You can cut large stickers in half and stick them separately but near each other. Take the smaller ones and stick two together. Cover the tablecloth with as many as you like. Remember that in this case it is hard to overdo; lots of stickers all over the table will look wonderful!

You can carry this theme even further: Cut the paper plates in half (use the 9-inch or larger plate) and place either one half or two separate halves at each place setting. Cut the cup in half horizontally. Do the same with the napkins. Put two of each plastic spoon and fork at each place setting.

4. Arrange the double toys. The match of this toy will be at the table serving as a place card—where the half birthday child will sit. These can be plastic doll shoes, matching playing cards, dice, matching colored crayons, etc. Place them on each plate or at the top of the plate (work out the seating arrangement with the birthday child).

5. Prepare the Complete the Name Game (good for children eight to twelve). With your child list the names of celebrities your child likes. Try to get a wide range of names from television, films, sports, literature, history, etc. Make a list of the first names only and xerox as many copies as there are guests. The guests must provide the last name of the "star." Get enough pencils and set aside.

6. If you want additional decorations, just double those you like. Place two balloons at each seat, hang crepe paper streamers everywhere, hang a Happy Birthday sign either cut in half horizontally or hang two signs to carry out the "double your fun" theme.

ACTIVITIES

1. Halfway Bingo • Take the cards in your inexpensive Bingo set and cut them in half. Play "Blackout" Bingo by covering the entire half card you hold.

2. Half A Pair Relay • The object of this game is to put on the matching sock and shoe and return to your starting line. The first to return with sock and shoe on wins.

Assemble those shoes and socks you prepared last week (it's more fun if the socks and shoes are large and unusual; the children will really get a laugh when they try to run with large shoes and see themselves in adult socks and shoes). Take two large cardboard boxes and put half the shoes in one box and half the socks in another. Place the two boxes at one end of the playroom, about 6 feet apart.

Have the children take off their own shoes and put them in a safe place. Give each child a sock and a shoe. Now line the children up at the starting line (which is on the other side of the room, away from the boxes of socks and shoes). At the signal, each child runs to the box of socks, finds the match, puts on the sock and returns to the starting line. He then runs over to the box of shoes, finds that match, puts on the shoe and returns to the starting line to win the game.

3. Complete the Name Game • This game is appropriate for ages eight to twelve. Divide the children into teams of twins according to their costumes. Pass out a list of celebrated first names you and your child have compiled. Get a timer and give the children 5 minutes to complete the list of names. Here are suggestions of possible names (but feel free to make up your own with your child):

Mary Lou	Robert
Jane	Debby
Lionel	Diana
Elizabeth	Ronald
Reggie	George
Barbra	Joe
Bill	Molly
Punky	Mickey
Michael	Karim
Cindy	Victoria

Phyllis Wolff loved the Half Birthday party idea so much that she gave it for an adult friend who was turning 39½. She figures it really took some of the pressure off becoming forty!

4. Slippery Slinky • This game is good for children four to seven years old. Have the children sit in a circle on the floor. Play one of your child's favorite songs on the record player or tape recorder and have the children pass a plastic Slinky (or other favorite toy) from hand to hand. When the music stops, the child left holding the Slinky is out. Whoever is the last one left in the circle wins.

5. Double Trivia • There are many games of Trivia on the market today, appropriate for ages eight to twelve. Choose one with your child. Divide the children into teams of twins. The winning team of twins might like their own set of Trivia cards.

6. Body Boggle (sometimes known as Twister) • This is a great game for all ages. You can buy Body Boggle at any toy store. In this game, children place various hands and feet on colors on a mat on the floor. It is a lot of fun and usually ends up in uproarious laughter. Try playing some funny circus-like music to add to the fun.

7. LUNCH

M • E • N • U

Half Sandwiches
Half Soft Pretzels
Half Apples or Bananas
Vivian's "Half a Round" Cake
Drinks in Half Cups

See the recipes on pages 224–25.

Any Ad Lib game works well. It is easy to play anytime—you don't have to plan it. Keep a pad of Ad Libs around, and whenever there is a lull in a party, suggest it.

ENTERTAINMENT

The games we have suggested should easily fill up two hours (that's including the food and gift-opening ceremony). For insurance, you might want to have another couple of pad and pencil games in reserve. Instead of playing all the games listed, you may choose to hire an amateur magician (a high school student is often a wonderful solution; he will most certainly be terrific, excited and easily able to relate to the children). Ask the magician if he can do tricks that are related to the "half" theme.

Yet another, more passive, form of entertainment would be to rent the videotape of the Disney classic *The Parent Trap*, a Hayley Mills film about twin girls.

FAVORS

Make sure you have at least two of each favor for each child. Don't try giving half of everything unless you want a lot of sad looks! It doesn't seem to work. You can give out two party bags per child, or you can use the bottoms and tops of gift boxes: simply place the favors for each child in half a box and cover with colored cellophane. Tie with two ribbons and you're done.

✳ A few weeks after Max Winkler's third birthday, his sister Zoe had hers. By the time this celebration was over, Max was feeling sad about his next birthday being months away. His parents, Henry and Stacey, decided he could have an Unbirthday. The deal was Max could choose his cake and his dinner, but there would be no gifts. The cake said "Happy Unbirthday Max," everyone sang "Happy Unbirthday to You," and Max was happy as could be!

MAD HATTER TEA PARTY

Ages 4–8

W e are not sure why so many people love tea parties. Maybe it is because Alice in Wonderland had a wonderful "Very Happy Unbirthday" with the Mad Hatter. Perhaps it is because tea parties seem so civilized, elegant and so grown-up; because mothers and their children, particularly daughters, seem to love to get "dressed up" and share in something so sophisticated and worldly. The reasons really don't matter; tea parties abound.

We love the juxtaposition of sophisticated elegance and madcap creativity, so our Mad Hatter Tea Party is a combination of both. Here the table will be set for an elegant tea; the activities will include hat decorating as well as playing various games; the children will dress in their Sunday best; and the mothers and dads will play "Maid" and "Butler." Get ready for a treat!

1 STAGE ONE

CHECKLIST

1. Prepare guest list
2. Prepare books for favors
3. Prepare invitations

TIP

Why wait for a birthday to have a party with your child? Invite her for a one-on-one tea party at home or an outing at her favorite restaurant. You will all remember this little "party" always.

1. Discuss the guest list with your child. This party works well for four children or twelve. You may be surprised at how nice it is to have girls and boys dressed up in their finest, looking forward to the surprises ahead.

2. The favors at this party will be the crazy hats that the children will make. For additional gifts, you may want to hand out paperback copies of *Alice in Wonderland, The Cat in the Hat* or *Hats for Sale*. For older children, give a copy of Carl Sandburg's *Rootabaga Stories*. Some of these books may have to be ordered from your local toy store or bookstore. So decide early enough to place your order.

3. Prepare the invitations.

INVITATION

This is our version of a Mary Poppins–type hat (see illustration). You can copy this design and have your child color each invitation in any color she likes. Then have her decorate each invitation. You can glue feathers, sequins, tiny ribbons and pieces of lace, and any other ideas you can find at your local sewing center or five-and-dime store. Each invitation can be different—that's the fun part. Work with your child. As usual, send the invitation in a padded or larger than usual envelope and decorate with crayons, markers or stickers.

The invitation can read:

WEAR YOUR BEST FOR
MARYANN'S
MAD HATTER TEA PARTY
Saturday, January 4
12–2 p.m.
at 666 Hartford Drive
RSVP 555-1234

STAGE TWO

1. Decorate the envelopes and send the invitations.

2. Discuss the games you want to play with your child. Give him some choices as to the kinds of hats he wants to have (he could also choose to have them all)—visors, straw hats, caps, felt berets, fedoras, etc. All of these can be found at inexpensive five-and-dime stores, Chinese stores, and hat emporiums. Buy one hat per child (and some doubles in case some kids want the same hat). Get the things you will need to decorate them: spray paint (great on the straw hats), beads, ribbons, plastic fruits, plastic and/or rhinestone necklaces and earrings, charms, netting and lace, paper streamers, sequins, and lots of glue and scissors.

CHECKLIST

1. Decorate envelopes and send invitations
2. Start collecting and/or buying hats and then accessories

STAGE THREE

1. Call the guests if they haven't responded.

2. Plan the menu now.

3. Show your child the dishes you plan to use. Try to set the table in as grown-up and elegant a manner as possible, without using your most precious (and breakable) china and silver. Choose a fancy (lace, for example) tablecloth. Use china (not necessarily your good Spode!) plates, cups and saucers—they will still be special to the children, if only because they are not paper plates! Discuss having flowers on the table, perhaps in tiny vases at each place setting. Plan on having a drink like ginger ale to serve in champagne glasses (you can use the plastic ones). Remember, it is important to create the mood and atmosphere of a grown-up party.

4. Get Polaroid film. You will want to take a picture of each child in his creation.

5. For children ages eight to twelve: Discuss the game Who Am I? with your child. Make a list of actresses and actors or other famous people the children would be likely to know and put them on index cards. These will be pinned to the back of each child's clothes and the child will have to guess who he is. Get safety pins.

CHECKLIST

1. Call RSVPs
2. Decide on menu
3. Prepare table accessories
4. Buy film
5. Prepare games
6. Borrow funny hats for decorations
7. Buy items for canopy
8. Get heart-shaped cookie cutter
9. Prepare maid and butler outfits

For children four to eight: You and your child cut out full-face pictures of people with hats on from magazines (a full-frame shot is one where the face and/or hat are at least three inches high). Now cut these in half and paste each half on a piece of colored paper 8½ by 11 inches. These will be ready for Fill in the Hat.

6. Borrow as many funny, unusual or old-fashioned hats as you can from friends and family members, the funnier, the better. These will be used as decoration around the house.

7. Buy streamers, masking tape, four ½-inch wooden dowels about 4 feet high (tomato stakes will do), and ribbons and balloons to create Susan Russell's dramatic and memorable canopy that has been a favorite at her children's parties for years. (See page 125.)

8. Buy a heart-shaped cookie cutter for the "tea" sandwiches.

9. Mom and Dad have an active role to play, beyond running the show. You have been elected to play the Maid and Butler at this tea party. For Mom, this means a black outfit with a white apron. If you have some sort of white bow or waitress-like crown, wear it. For Dad, if you have a tuxedo, please wear it. If not, a black suit with a bow tie will do. Try serving with a towel draped over your arm.

✳ Sandra Brown's daughter Alex got the flu on her birthday. The party was canceled, but Sandra was adamant about not canceling the celebration. She placed little presents all around Alex's room and decorated it with balloons, flowers and a birthday banner. It worked so well that she has continued to decorate Alex's room on each birthday.

4 STAGE FOUR

1. Buy the food for the menu. You will need: ladyfingers, peanut butter, cucumbers, ready-sliced bread of your choice, tea, Hot Apple Cider, and the ingredients for the Proper Sugar Cookies and Mad Hatter Absolutely Sinful M&M Birthday Cake. Remember that for the cucumber hearts you will need a heart-shaped cookie cutter, and for the cake you will need about 3 cups of M&Ms and a 3-inch satin ribbon, brightly colored, about 3 feet long.

2. Bake the cookies and cake. Refrigerate.

3. You are about to create a table neither you nor your child will ever forget. Mark our words, years from now, when your child turns to you and says, "Mom, Dad, remember the time you made that canopy for the table at the tea party? That was fabulous!"

This is a canopy that was created by Susan Russell for the birthday parties of her daughters, Megan and Cory.

CHECKLIST

1. Buy food
2. Bake cookies and cake
3. Make canopy
4. Set table
5. Make banner

Making the Tea Party Canopy:

First fasten a stick (a dowel or tomato stake) to each corner of the dining room table with masking or packing tape. Cover each stake with colored streamers (just wind them around the stick as you would a maypole). Using strong mailing tape, tape lots of long streamers from the ceiling over the center of the table to the top of each stick, creating a maypole effect. Let the streamers hang once you tape them to the tops of the poles. Blow up the balloons and attach three or four to the top of each stick or pole. You can add ribbons to each pole for added texture and color. The result, as pictured below, is dramatic and beautiful and will absolutely make this tea party unforgettable!

4. Now set the table. Use china teacups and saucers, a lace tablecloth or lace doilies, cloth napkins and a china teapot. Place individual vases at each place setting, but wait to insert the flowers until tomorrow or have one flower centerpiece.

5. There are some funny things you can do to put everyone in the Mad Hatter mood. If it is a birthday party and you want to put up a banner, design one with humor. Draw funny hats all over it. If you like, you can write Happy Birthday with some of the letters in the shape of hats. Decorate one hat in the silliest designs imaginable and hang it on the front door. Take those funny hats you borrowed and hang them everywhere in the party room.

✳ Our friend Suzanne Jeffers has a tea party with her three-year-old daughter Courtney whenever they can. It's a real Tea for Two. They set the table with china, have a light tea with sugar and cream, some favorite cookies, and then read the book *Six Days, Twenty Three Cats, Forty Five Mice and One Hundred and Sixteen Spiders* out loud to each other, taking turns pretending to be characters from the book. It's a very special time for both mother and daughter, one neither seems willing to give up.

5 STAGE FIVE

CHECKLIST

1. Make food and set out on table
2. Dress as Maid and Butler
3. Prepare hat-decorating table

1. Prepare the Cucumber Hearts or Ladyfinger Sandwiches. Make some Hot Apple Cider and Hot Tea and keep warm in a thermos.

Put the cookies on a platter. Remove the cake from the refrigerator and set on the counter.

2. Dress as the Maid and Butler. Be sure to greet everyone at the door in your costume.

3. Prepare table with hats and items for decorating them.

ACTIVITIES

1. Decorating Hats • As the kids walk in the front door, direct them to a table laden with hats and paraphernalia for decorating them. This starts the children in an activity even while everyone is waiting for other guests to arrive. Have one hat already decorated just so they can see what is possible. Encourage the kids to be wild in their designs. Have plastic fruits, fish, cars and other figures that they can hang from the brim. Let them go for it!

2. Picture-Taking • Because the children are so photogenic in their "dress-up" clothes and their funny hats, this is a good time to make picture-taking an activity. Splurge and get lots of extra film for the fun ahead. First, as each child is done decorating his hat, take a Polaroid picture of him in it. Next have the children pose in funny positions with their hats on. Now you can take serious "grown-up" shots of the children in full dress. If you like you can have the birthday child take the pictures, or at least a couple of them. She can also be "in charge" of the photo-taking session, picking which child has his picture taken first and last. You can also make the birthday child the "director" of the photo session. Have her give instructions—"smile," "be sad," "be mad," "be silly," etc.—to each child. In short, be creative and make this photo session a lot of fun. Also take a group photograph for the birthday child. If you like, you can reproduce this later and send it to all the children.

3. Who Am I? • Take those index cards with the names of famous people that you made two weeks before. Attach a card to the back of each child's shirt or dress (pinning is best). Thus the children do not know "who they are." Now begin the

Jean Kennedy Smith always remembers mothers on the children's birthdays; she sends her mother flowers on her own birthday every year.

✱ Lynda Johnson Robb's favorite party was the graduation tea she gave with her daughter Lucinda. The mothers dressed as their daughters and the daughters dressed as their mothers. Lynda served ginger ale for the "moms" and Coke for the "daughters" in crystal champagne glasses. They sat down to tea sandwiches and cookies at an elegant table for an unforgettable gathering.

game. Each child asks questions that need a "yes" or "no" answer to try to guess who she is. The first child to guess who she is wins first prize, the second wins second prize, and so on.

4. Fill in the Hat • Hand out the magazine photos of people in hats that you have cut in half and pasted on a large sheet of paper. Give each child this sheet and some markers and let him draw the other half of the face and hat. When done, display all the drawings.

5. TEA TIME

See the recipes on pages 225–27.

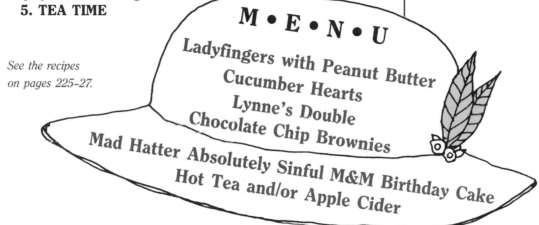

M • E • N • U

Ladyfingers with Peanut Butter
Cucumber Hearts
Lynne's Double
Chocolate Chip Brownies
Mad Hatter Absolutely Sinful M&M Birthday Cake
Hot Tea and/or Apple Cider

ENTERTAINMENT

This tea party is full of activities that should take you at least two hours. In the "more rather than less" spirit of planning, you might prepare another activity or two. Dancing to the birthday child's favorite music might be fun. Or they can act out a scene from *Alice in Wonderland*, such as the "Mad Tea-Party." There are some wonderful parts the children can play—the March Hare, the Hatter, Alice, Dormouse. Can you imagine such lines as "Why, you might just as well say that 'I see what I eat' is the same thing as 'I eat what I see!'" or "Twinkle, twinkle, little bat! How I wonder what you're at! Up above the world you fly, Like a tea-tray in the sky," coming out of the mouths of your babes? All you need for this is a xeroxed copy of the Mad Hatter Tea chapter from *Alice in Wonderland*.

FAVORS

These smiling children have their funny hats and their precious photographs of themselves. For additional favors, give out the paperback books you ordered weeks ago: *Alice in Wonderland*, *The Cat in the Hat*, or Carl Sandburg's *Rootabaga Stories*.

Ages 4–12

W as there ever a child who didn't want to be a magician? At least for a day? Magic is childhood, and childhood is magic. And for those of us children, young and old, who have always been entranced by magic, this party is a special treat.

1 | STAGE ONE

1. Prepare the guest list. This party is flexible enough to be given for young children and older ones.

2. Make and send the invitations.

INVITATION

The invitation for this party is a balloon. Buy balloons in various colors, blow them up and fasten with rubber bands. Write the invitation on them with permanent markers. When done, deliver in your neighborhood.

If you prefer sending the invitations, buy Adam's magic tricks and send them with the invitation attached. Ask each guest to learn to perform this trick and bring it with him.

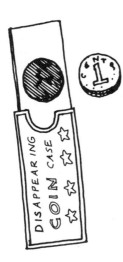

DISAPPEARING COIN CASE

COME TO ANDY'S
MYSTERIOUS MAGICAL PARTY
on
Saturday, January 18th
from 12 - 2 p.m.
at
555 Pershing Drive RSVP 555-1234

3. You can make this a costume party by asking the children to come dressed as magicians or fortune-tellers. Imagine a house full of children dressed in these exotic and elegant costumes and you can tell what a fun party this is going to be!

4. Convince a member of your family or a friend to perform magic, or find a high school student who does magic and loves to perform. Then recruit yet another friend to rise to the challenge and come dressed as a fortune-teller. The latter needs no experience. You can get a "crystal" ball (Magic Eight Balls are sold in toy stores) and/or a Ouija board; you furnish the children's zodiac signs (you can also prepare the fortunes); and he can make up the palm and card readings. All this person needs is an elaborate, flashy costume to set the mood, and a great sense of humor.

CHECKLIST

1. Prepare guest list
2. Make and send invitations
3. Decide on costume party
4. Select entertainers

STAGE TWO

2

1. Call RSVPs. Be sure to ask the parents for their children's birth dates so you can get their zodiac signs.

2. Start collecting the decorations. You will need: top hats, wands, playing cards (large and small), multicolored scarves (borrow these—you'll need at least a dozen); inexpensive magic sets (Adam's Magic makes many magic tricks that you can buy individually in most toy stores. Pre-select tricks that are appropriate for your age group so young children won't be frustrated by tricks that are too difficult for them).

3. Prepare the games. You will need:

- rolls of pennies for the Magical Mystery Tour (get enough pennies so each child can find at least twenty); containers to hold the pennies—these could be the "favor" bags (top hats, velvet pouches, plastic bags or colored paper bags with the children's names on them)
- T-shirts and a compilation of the signs of the zodiac (you can find these on many calendars)
- permanent fabric markers and/or glitter pens
- lots of old clothes, hats, boas, inexpensive jewelry, shoes and gloves for the Magical Relay

4. Look over the menu. If you want to substitute any dishes, this is the time to make such changes.

5. Prepare the favors. Some suggestions include top hats (unless the kids have come as magicians), magic wands, decks of cards, magic rocks, individual magic tricks, books on magic.

For a change of pace, you can set up a "Magic Store" named after your child. The children will gather pennies on the Magical Mystery Tour. Have them save the pennies to "buy" their favors at the store at the end of the party.

3 STAGE THREE

1. Decorate the party room and table. Place top hats and wands on the table. Put large and small playing cards everywhere. Decorate everything in black and red (you can buy paper plates, cloths, cups, etc. in these colors).

Gather the scarves. Fasten one inside a top hat and place it on the table. Tie the rest to each other and string the line of scarves across the room, up to the ceiling and down again—anywhere you can to create a magical effect.

Take some of the inexpensive magic tricks and set them around the table. Along with the meal the kids will be trying out their tricks.

2. Make the food and bake the cake.

3. Speak with your entertainers. Confirm their time of arrival. You may want to start out with the magician, then play the games, and then have the fortune-teller arrive.

4. If you are setting up the Magic Store for the favors, do it today.

5. There are a couple of great magic tricks that we learned years ago from Mr. Wizard. You can put these in the center of the table and we guarantee they'll be the talk of this already "full" party (as well as the schoolyard tomorrow). You will have to set the tricks up as kids sit down to eat, but they are simple to do. Just prepare the items you will need today: a glass salad bowl, baking soda, macaroni in different shapes, vinegar, a tall empty wine bottle, and some food coloring.

6. Have your child clean the pennies you collected. Combine 4 tablespoons of salt and ½ cup vinegar in a bowl. Throw in the pennies and stir. Now wipe them clean and save until tomorrow. In the morning you can hide the pennies for the hunt.

ACTIVITIES

Have the magician start entertaining the children as they arrive. He starts by performing a few simple tricks for the birthday child and continues as the guests come in. Your child can be the assistant.

1. Magical Mystery Tour • You have hidden the pennies your child cleaned yesterday. Give the children their personalized "favor" bags and let them find the pennies.

2. Penny Magic • Here's another game you can play with the pennies. Make the birthday child the hero of this game by anointing her the "Penny Magician" and telling her the secret ahead of time.

Pick five pennies with different dates on them. Place the pennies in a top hat and ask one of the kids to pick one penny and look at the date. Have the group pass the penny around until each person has checked the date. Promptly and quickly put all the pennies into the hat and shake them up. Have the Penny Magician reach into the hat and pull out the chosen penny.

The secret? The Penny Magician knows which penny was chosen because copper absorbs heat, so the penny everyone has handled will be warm. Once everyone knows how the magic is done, let all the children have a turn being the Penny Magician.

3. Fortune-Telling T-Shirts • Arrange a table with markers and the T-shirts. Give each child a shirt and a drawing or picture of his sign of the zodiac. He can then draw that sign on his own shirt and write his name on it. If you can find zodiac transfers, try those.

✳ Marc Gilbar decided to dress as a magician when he was the "assistant" at his magic party. Annie bought an inexpensive costume of tie and tails and a magician's cape at a local toy store.

4. Magical Relay • At one end of the room, place a box filled with the old clothes and accessories you collected. Now divide the children into two teams. The object is to have two children (one child from each team) run across the room to the box and put on three pieces of clothing of their choice, run back to their team, take the clothes off and pass them on to the next kid on their team. These kids then have to put on these clothes, run across the room and put on another three pieces of clothing, run back to their team, and so on.

5. Fortune-Teller • Have her entertain the kids by telling their fortunes. She can use their zodiac signs, do palm and card reading, and even try tea leaves.

6. Centerpieces • This activity is for you. While the kids are being entertained by the fortune-teller, you can get the magical centerpieces ready.

1. In a large glass salad bowl (one with straight sides works best), put 6 cups of water and 3 tablespoons of baking soda. Mix until the soda dissolves. Put 1 cup of uncooked macaroni in the bowl. The pieces will sink to the bottom. Add the food coloring and stir. When the children are ready to sit down to eat, stir in ½ cup of vinegar. The chemical reaction will cause the bubbles to form on the ends of the macaroni and the pieces will float to the top. When the action slows down, simply add more vinegar.

2. Put the wine bottle in another large glass bowl. Pour 2 cups of water into the bottle and add 1 tablespoon of baking soda and a few drops of liquid soap detergent. When the children are ready to sit down at the table, pour 3 to 4 tablespoons of vinegar into the bottle. Tiny soap bubbles will foam up and over the top of the bottle. To keep it going, just add more soap and vinegar.

TIP

At the end of the party, if you still need to occupy the children, bring out a deck of cards. Some favorite games include Fish, War, Old Maid and Gin Rummy.

7. MAGIC LUNCH

M • E • N • U

Pita Roll-Ups with
Surprise Fillings
Chips
Soda and Punch
Hidden Secrets
Magic Cake

See the recipes on pages 227–28.

FAVORS

You can set up the Magic Store where the children "buy" their favors with their pennies. Some suggestions include individual magic tricks, magic rocks, playing cards, top hats, wands, magic books and any of Mr. Wizard's books on science experiments.

✳ Amy Carter's third birthday party was held at the Governor's Mansion in Atlanta, Georgia, just before Halloween. Her mother, Rosalynn, had red capes made for the guests so each child could be a Little Red Riding Hood. They all "dressed up" in Amy's room, then took the elevator, which was decked out with branches, leaves and twigs to resemble the forest, downstairs. Your "mansion" may not have an elevator, but try decorating the hallway in a similar manner for a walk through the woods!

MAKE-UP PARTY

Ages 8 and up

If you've ever caught your daughter sneaking a look in your mirror at her newly painted red lips, you'll know what we mean when we say every little girl has a yen to try Mom's make-up. While we may not encourage young girls to wear make-up, trying it does seem like a lot of fun as part of playing "dress up." For all the young girls who can't wait to see what make-up does to their lovely faces, here's a party where they can "paint" to their heart's content!

1 STAGE ONE

1. Put together the guest list. Obviously, this party lends itself to being an all-girl party.

2. Make and send invitations.

INVITATION

Your daughter will have no trouble finding pictures of models in magazines that she can cut out and glue to an 8½- by 11-inch sheet of paper. Then she can write the party invitation information on the front. Mail in a regular business-size envelope.

3. Begin to buy and collect the make-up and accessories you will need. Buy inexpensive hypo-allergenic products at beauty supply, discount or five-and-dime stores—and buy lots of them in different shades and colors. Buy or collect blush-on make-up, concealer, eye shadow, mascara (one for each), eyelash curlers, eye pencils, lipstick (one for each), make-up remover, contouring cream, tissues, cotton balls, alcohol, nail polish and nail polish remover, brushes (make-up and hair), combs, colored

CHECKLIST

1. Make up your guest list
2. Make and send invitations
3. Start collecting make-up and accessories
4. Prepare decorations (area for salon)
5. Arrange for extra help

TIP

Rebecca Bloom had six twelve-year-olds over for her make-up party (they even slept over) when she started seventh grade. It was not her birthday—it was a great way to get acquainted with her new classmates. Giving a party for no special occasion (but for such a nice reason) is just as much fun as celebrating a birthday.

DON'T BLUSH!
come to
ELIZABETH'S
MAKE-UP PARTY!
at
Elizabeth's
Beauty Salon

666 MOUNTAIN DRIVE
Saturday, February 8
4-6 p.m.

TO MAKE YOUR
APPOINTMENT
Call 555-1234

mousse for hair, glittery hair bows and clips, hair dryers, curling iron, hot rollers, lots of mirrors—and maybe even more!

4. Turn your home into a Beauty Salon. You can use the kitchen, bathrooms or a playroom that has outlets and where you can place mirrors. Cover these areas with plastic tablecloths and have lots of paper towels around. You might want to get plastic smocks for the girls (sold at beauty supply centers).

5. You will need adult supervision. Also find some high schoolers who know and love to "do" make-up and hair. They will relish the chance to put make-up on the younger girls! Moreover, having several "older beauty operators" around will give the atmosphere of a real beauty parlor. If you have six to eight guests, get at least five or six "beauty operators."

STAGE TWO 2

1. Call the guests who haven't responded.

2. Go over the menu. Buy the products you will need now.

3. Beside having their make-up and hair done, we have scheduled other activities. Prepare for these now:

- For Scrambled Words, you will need to list (or copy) our words so each girl has a copy. They will each also need pencils.

- For Crazy Heads, you will need Styrofoam heads (the ones stores use to display hats and wigs), inexpensive false eyelashes, earrings, lipsticks, markers, curly chenille or thick yarn and spray paint. If you have a source or two that will lend you wigs, you've got it made! (Whatever happened to all those wigs that made an appearance in the 60's? Can they be found in the back of a friend's closet?) The Styrofoam heads are available in beauty supply stores.

4. Discuss the favors with your daughter. The girls will be taking home photos, the Crazy Heads they have made and some make-up. You may also want to give them little make-up bags in which to carry any of the products they've been given.

5. In addition to cutting out models for the invitation, your daughter might want to paste such cut-outs on the paper tablecloth.

CHECKLIST

1. Call RSVPs
2. Check menu
3. Prepare the other activities
4. Discuss favors
5. Decorate with magazine cut-outs

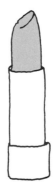

3 STAGE THREE

1. Prepare the Roast Beef Wrappers, Vegetable Ladies and Ice Cream Cake.

2. In the Beauty Salon area, set out all the hair and make-up accessories. Set up the make-up in plastic containers. Have lots of tissue boxes everywhere.

3. Set the table. Use paper everything.

4. The taking of pictures is important at this party because you will want "before" and "after" shots of the girls. If you have an instant camera, use it so the girls can take these photos home with them.

5. On a large table (or on the dining room table when lunch is done), be prepared to set out the Crazy Heads and their accessories and the Scrambled Words papers and pencils.

ACTIVITIES

1. Make-Up and Hair at the Beauty Salon • This is self-explanatory. The teenagers do the make-up and hair of the girls. If you like, you can set up an "Appointment Desk" with someone to "schedule" who is doing whose make-up and hair.

2. LUNCH • After the hair-dos and make-up is a good time to have lunch, and do the other activities later.

CHECKLIST

1. Prepare food
2. Decorate and arrange the Beauty Salon
3. Set table
4. Prepare cameras
5. Collect items for games/and favors

TIP

Take a hint from the airlines and serve lunch or dinner on Styrofoam trays. The kids will love the change, and the trays are easily disposable.

M • E • N • U
Roast Beef Wrappers
Vegetable Ladies
Ice Cream Cake

See the recipes on page 228.

3. Scrambled Words • Give the girls a sheet of paper with the scrambled words having to do with make-up. Give them a time limit to figure out the puzzle.

1.	HBSUL NO	BLUSH ON
2.	HRSBU	BRUSH
3.	YEE WDHASO	EYE SHADOW
4.	SPKIICTL	LIPSTICK
5.	DWOERP	POWDER
6.	HEESALY LURECR	EYELASH CURLER
7.	CRAMASA	MASCARA
8.	MRCAE	CREAM
9.	SRAELECN	CLEANSER
10.	KPEMUA	MAKE-UP

4. Crazy Heads • Place the Styrofoam heads on the table. In small bins, hand out the various accessories you bought for these. The object is for the girls to decorate the heads with the eyelashes, paints, yarn for hair, etc. They get to take these home.

FAVORS

"Before" and "After" Polaroids, the Crazy Heads they made and make-up bags filled with miscellaneous make-up.

❋ Ever consider giving a surprise party for your child? Lynne Sprecher gave a surprise breakfast party for daughter Thea's eighth birthday. Although Lynne told the mothers of her plans weeks before, the kids only found out the night before the party. Lynne sent Thea out with her dad to get bagels while a dozen friends arrived in their pajamas and slippers and hid in the closet. When Thea returned she was stunned to discover her friends waiting to share a breakfast of pancakes, doughnuts and strawberries. This simple and delightful party lasted from 8:00 a.m. to 10:00 a.m. and is still the talk of LA!

❋ When Maryann Pope gave a tea party for her daughter Alex's eighth birthday, she decorated a sun visor the day before and displayed it so the guests could envision the possibilities for great and unusual designs. Try this with the Styrofoam head for this party.

START

Olympics

Olympics

FINISH

OLYMPICS PARTY

Ages 6 and up

[O] lympic fever never goes away. It doesn't have to be the year of the Olympics to have children of all ages simply crazy about anything to do with the Games. Try mentioning having an Olympic party, where the children compete in activities and get medals and ribbons in closing ceremonies, and if your child's eyes light up then this is the party to give.

Discuss the Olympics; you can talk about the Games, the athletes, and how exciting the process of competition is to both the competitors and the spectators. Remind your child about the festivities of the Games—the music, the parades, the banners and memorabilia. If you have any books or magazines about any Olympics, share them together to remind everyone how exciting and extraordinary the Olympic Games have been throughout history.

1 STAGE ONE

CHECKLIST

1. Assess backyard
2. Make guest list
3. Prepare invitations
4. Go over list of games

TIP

Buy plastic squeeze bottles at a beauty supply store and fill with water. When your athletes are parched for a drink, just squeeze the water into their open mouths.

1. As this is an outdoor party, it is difficult to have it without a backyard, unless you have a public park that has a separate area you can take over for an afternoon. Trying to hold the Olympics in your high-rise apartment is inconvenient and probably impossible. At this time assess the playing area you have as you go over the events list. If you need to clear your backyard or move some lawn furniture around, this is the time to do it. Defining your space may make the difference between being able to have an Olympics and choosing another party. You may be able to incorporate some of your existing features into the events. For example, we have designed an obstacle course that you create, but if you have a little hill or a low bush or fence, you may want to include it in your own obstacle course. If you have a large playroom and no backyard, you can adapt some of these activities for an indoor Olympics.

2. Put your guest list together. If you have the room in your backyard, or particularly if you have this party in the park, and if you have sufficient adult supervision, you can invite many children of all ages. For Olympic festivities, the more is really the merrier.

3. Make your invitations.

INVITATION

The invitation is a winning ribbon. You can order such ribbons from Recognition Enterprises (see page 146 for the address) with the party information printed on them. Or, to make them yourself:

Buy 3-inch-wide satin ribbon in any color (the bright colors—gold, blue, red, green, purple—work the best). You will need a 5-inch length for each invitation. Also buy some gold seals in any stationery store (you will need one for each invitation and one for each envelope). Cut the 5-inch strip of ribbon to a V shape at the bottom (see illustration) and glue one gold seal in the center (don't just lick it and expect it to stick—it won't! Use a strong glue to ensure that it won't fall off in the mail).

Now type out a message similar to the following on paper. You will then xerox this for as many invitations as you need, cut out 2½- by 3-inch pieces and staple each on the reverse side of the ribbons (not on the side with the gold seal). And that's the invitation!

Put each invitation in a padded or heavy paper envelope. Place another gold seal on the outside of the envelope near the address.

4. Look over the list of games we have. They are a lot of fun and will motivate your family to begin preparations for your own Olympics. If you and your child have any other ideas for games and competitions, by all means plan them.

JOYCE'S OLYMPIC PARTY

Run, Jump, Crawl, Throw and Win!

FOR:
WHEN:
WHERE:
AT:
RSVP:

WEAR SWEATS, SNEAKERS AND A SMILE

STAGE TWO 2

1. Send the invitations; be sure to decorate the envelopes.

2. This is a good time to start collecting the items you will need for the games. You may be able to do all this two weeks before the party, but if you start early, you will have enough time to search for items you don't have and borrow or order those you can't buy easily.

CHECKLIST

1. Send invitations
2. Collect Olympic accessories

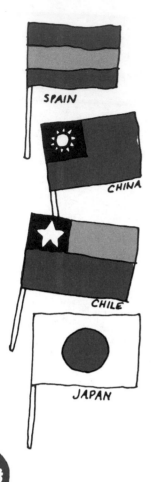

SPAIN

CHINA

CHILE

JAPAN

TIP

If you are concerned about competition among the children, or if you've invited more than 20 children, forget the First-, Second- and Third-prize ribbons. Instead, buy three yards of each of seven different colors of ribbon (one color per event) and cut into 2- to 3-inch lengths. Attach a safety pin to each. When each child completes an event, give him the ribbon for that event. When the game is over, each happy child will have seven different ribbons pinned to his chest!

You will need:

- Plenty of winning ribbons. Check at your local sports store; they often carry ribbons with First Place, Second Place, etc., printed across the front. They also have ribbons with lined paper attached to the back where you can fill out the name of the winner and what he won the ribbon for. You can also order ribbons from Recognition Enterprises, 15450 Cabrito Rd., Van Nuys, CA 91406. Ask for Susan McGraw, (818) 997-0736. Stock ribbons (without card in back) are 30 cents each; with card in back, 50 cents each. Allow two weeks to order; 25 is the minimum amount. Pins are included.

  The ribbon with paper attached to the back is perfect for giving ribbons to the children who didn't place in the competition (and can also be used as the invitation). Be creative; give ribbons for longest legs, trying hard (you can give a lot of these!), best coordinated, greatest uniform, best performance, terrific throw, etc. You can easily make these as well.
- Plastic "Gold" medals (they look just like Olympic Medals). If you can't find them at your local toy store, make them with large gold seals.
- A stopwatch (you can get extra inexpensive plastic stopwatches for prizes/favors)
- A play tunnel—the kind you buy for toddlers (you can find it at most toy stores)
- Old pillowcases (you'll never sleep on these again!)
- At least five Nerf or Wiffle balls
- Binoculars
- A tricycle
- Miscellaneous items: Scarves, several tape measures, a couple of Frisbees, three brooms, a plastic bucket, a couple of empty milk cartons, string, red tape (to mark the finish lines) and plastic straws wrapped in paper (that's our Javelin Throw). For the Nerf Ball Toss, you'll need three large cartons—one marked 5 points, one 10 points, one 15 points—and the Nerf balls.
- Lots and lots of film! Assign one person to be in charge of taking pictures continually throughout the party.
- Very important: It will really make a difference if you can get hold of a record or tape of the theme from the Olympics (or the theme from the movie *Chariots of Fire*). Nothing gets a crowd going better than music!

STAGE THREE

1. Call any guests who haven't responded.

2. Get a large white sheet and some acrylic paints (you can use brushes or spray paint). Paint "Joyce's Olympics Birthday" in large letters. If you prefer, and if you can get hold of one, you can use a sheet from a roll of butcher paper as a banner.

To order a personalized banner, write Computer Readings Corp., 22019 Vanowen St., Canoga Park, CA 91303, or call (800) 556-0670.

3. Many party, stationery, flag or banner stores carry paper flags from various countries. You'll need a different one to pin on each child. They also make wonderful decorations! Get them in different sizes. The large ones can be placed around the backyard. The smaller ones can be given out at the ceremonies, on the sandwiches or with the favors. Tiny paper flags on toothpicks are wonderful on the Hero Cupcakes.

4. Organize the games at this time. It will make you feel less anxious and more secure about what will happen at the party. The easiest way to organize the games is to take a piece of graph paper (or any accounting paper) and on the left-hand side, in a column, list the name and country of each guest/competitor. At the top of the page, running horizontally across the page, list the games. You can xerox a few of these for each adult who will be helping you. During the games, you can fill in the scores of the children (first, second or third, etc.). Here is a sample of "Joyce's Olympic Score Sheet":

	DASH	JUMP	OBSTACLE	FRISBEE	NERF	TOSS	JAVELIN
US *REMY*							
UK *LISA*							
SPAIN *VIVIAN*							
CHILE *WYNNE*							
JAPAN *ALEX*							
CHINA *MEGHAN*							
INDIA *MARC*							

If you have more than 20 guests, divide the kids into teams with country names and give prizes to each team member.

5. Be sure you have a clipboard, pencil and whistle for each adult.

6. Finalize your menu. You will need a cookie cutter in the shape of a star for the sandwiches. You can get the ingredients for the Award-Winning All-Stripe Jell-O, but don't make it until the day before. You will be serving lunch as a picnic, so prepare paper plates, cups, napkins and anything else you may need.

4 | STAGE FOUR

There will be enough to do the day before the party, so do yourself a favor and prepare at least a couple of things two days before.

1. Make the Award-Winning All-Stripe Jello-O the day before.

2. Bake the cupcakes. You can decorate them with either an Olympic flag or a country flag. If this is a birthday party, you may want to make an extra large cupcake and write the birthday child's name on it.

Make the Champion Sandwiches, wrap and refrigerate.

3. If you have not made your Olympic banner, do it today.

4. Gather together all the things you will need for the games. Call your adult or teenage helpers and ask them to arrive early on the day of the party to help you set up the games.

ACTIVITIES

About half an hour before the party, gather the adults who have agreed to help you and go over the games with them. Hand out clipboards, pencils and "Joyce's Olympic Score Sheets." Have the ribbons ready (decide on which colors will be used for First, Second and Third places). Organize the things you will need for each game so you won't have to stop the activities to find anything.

There are seven events, with the Obstacle Course having six events of its own. Each child begins with the 10-Yard Dash and ends with the Javelin Throw. When a child has finished the first event, he goes on to the second and the second child

CHECKLIST

1. Make Jell-O
2. Bake cupcakes and make sandwiches
3. Make banner
4. Gather items for games

TIP

Mary Ellen Geisser always writes down the schedule of activities and sticks it in her pocket. It makes her feel more secure!

148

begins the first. The score is cumulative; the child who does the best in all events wins first place. We suggest that there be three big winners—First, Second and Third places. You can give a certain number of points to First, Second and Third places. Then you can give all the other children those extra ribbons for prizes you made up. The goal is to give a ribbon to every single child who participated in the games. As long as each child wins something, everyone will be happy and feel that he's had a fabulous time. And isn't that what the Olympics is all about?

If this is a birthday party, be sure to remember to give the birthday child some extra duties. She can play "referee"; she can always start first in the different events; she can keep time with the stopwatch.

As the children arrive, pin their country flags on their shirts.

THE EVENTS:

1. 10-Yard Dash • Each child has to get to the 10-yard line with his feet in a pillowcase. Use the stopwatch—the fastest time wins.

2. Long Jump • The person who jumps the farthest wins first place. No pillowcases here!

3. Frisbee Toss • Hit the empty milk carton with a Frisbee. Give each child three chances.

If you have a portable cassette player, play either the Olympic theme or any other music of that type as you begin the events. (The theme from *The Lone Ranger*—the *William Tell* Overture—is great!)

4. Olympic Obstacle Course • You need a stopwatch to time each child as she goes through the course. Encourage the children to cheer each other on.

a) Crawl through the play tunnel.
b) Hop over three broomsticks.
c) Roll on the ground to:
d) Binoculars and string. (Take a 6-foot length of string and fasten it into the ground, as taut as possible. Take a pair of binoculars, turn them upside down, look down into them and walk a straight line.)
e) Crawl on all fours to where the tricycle is parked.
f) Ride the tricycle to the finish line (make this at least 20 feet if possible; let them go a ways on the bike, with everyone cheering them on).

5. Nerf Ball Toss • Line up the boxes that say 5, 10 and 15 points on them about 5, 8 and 10 feet away from a starting line, respectively. The object is to throw a Nerf ball into the carton marked with the highest number of points.

6. Javelin Throw • Each child stands behind a starting line. Give each a paper-covered straw, with the paper still on. The trick is to blow the straw and shoot the paper the farthest. The one who gets it the farthest gets the highest points, the second farthest the second highest points, etc. For a variation, the child can simply throw the straws with his hands.

7. Three-Legged Relay • This is the last event in these Olympics, so wait until all the children have completed everything else before you start. Now divide the children into two teams. The object is to take two people from each team, tie their legs together with a scarf and have them get to the finish line (make it about 20 feet, if possible). The two who have the fastest time get three points, the second two, etc.

8. Medal Awards Ceremony • Have three boxes ready. If you can, find three different-size boxes, at three different heights. Play the Olympic theme. Award the First, Second and Third place-winning ribbons. Then hand out all the other ribbons, having each child come up to the platforms. Encourage lots of cheers. Make sure you take a picture of each child receiving his ribbon.

Have the birthday child lead a parade for opening and closing ceremonies, holding a flag or torch. Have the children march to the Olympic theme

When all the medals are awarded, have a parade to the music.

9. OLYMPIC LUNCH

M • E • N • U

Champion Sandwiches
Popcorn
Award-Winning
All-Stripe Jell-O
Hero Cupcakes
Drinks

See the recipes on pages 229–30.

FAVORS

Each child gets her ribbon and a picture of herself getting the ribbon (and any others you have of the child during the games). You can give out additional favors if you like. Our suggestions would include sweatbands, visors, inexpensive plastic stopwatches, Olympic stickers or banners, flags from different countries or Nerf balls.

 Art and Ann Buchwald have held an annual family egg hunt at Easter time for years, first for their children and now for their grandchildren. One year the hunt developed a new twist: The family colored the eggs, and Art carefully hid them, including one he sprayed gold (and for which he promised to pay $5 to the winner). But the tradition of the golden egg ended the year child after child turned in golden eggs. Art soon ran out of $5 bills and had to write checks (while the friends who had done him in by hiding extra eggs had a good laugh).

ORCHESTRA PARTY

Ages 4 and up

E very parent knows the importance of music in our children's lives. From the time that we sing them "The itsy bitsy spider went up the water spout" to the time that they sing, "Beat it! Just beat it!" to us, music permeates their lives. But how many of our children know how music is written? How many know what instruments make up an orchestra, how the sounds of individual instruments make up one entire orchestral sound, or how instruments are made and how they make music?

Show a child a guitar and he immediately wants to play it. Show him how to make a guitar and you've got not only his attention but a child who is eager to learn and to play. Put a bunch of children together to make instruments and to play them and you've got—you guessed it—an Orchestra party!

This party works for children of all ages, up to at least twelve. For two- to four-year-olds, you may want to buy simple instruments and have them play them and sing along. The older children can take part in the complete party.

1 STAGE ONE

1. You're going to need help with this party. It is easy to organize and to direct, but you will need someone who knows something about music so she can answer questions and teach the children something about orchestras and how music is made. You can call your local symphony or band, or get a music student from the high school. If you know any music teachers, ask them. If you have a relative who is a musician, corral him to help out. He will enjoy the experience as much as the kids.

2. Check your best sticker outlet to see if they have stickers in the shape of musical notes and instruments. Buy a lot; you'll use some on the envelopes and the rest for decoration at the party.

3. Prepare the invitation. Ours is in the shape of a ticket to a concert. You can xerox this ticket on colored paper and then cut it out. The ticket could read:

☆ ADMIT ☆
Tracy Strauss
MARCH | 12TH | 1:00pm
TO
JONATHAN'S PHILHARMONIC ORCHESTRA PARTY
come to one performance only
for further ticket information and to R.S.V.P: CALL 555-5555

Put the invitation in a colored envelope. Cover with the stickers in the shape of notes or have your child draw notes on the envelopes with colored markers.

CHECKLIST

1. Arrange for someone to help you
2. Get stickers in the shape of musical notes
3. Prepare invitations

STAGE TWO

2

1. If the invitations have not yet been sent, do it now. Make your RSVP list.

2. Buy and/or collect the following for making the instruments (you will be making at least two of each instrument): coffee cans, beans, metal soda cans, uncooked rice, unpopped popcorn, plastic milk bottles (save the caps), plastic graters, wooden spoons, plastic string or rope, metal pot lids, kazoos, bells, metal spoon and drinking glasses, shoeboxes (with covers), rubber bands and metal pipes (buy eight of these at a plumbing supply store—¼-inch plumbing pipe would be fine); have them cut the pipes in four different lengths—two would be 12 inches long, two 9 inches long, two 6 inches long and two 4 inches long. Have them also drill a hole at one end of each so you can hang them).

You can buy children's instruments for two- to four-year-olds to play, or for prizes or favors, at most toy stores. A good collection includes tambourines, maracas, castanets, harmonicas and handbells.

3. Call local record stores and ask if they have any records that they plan to throw away. Very often record stores are happy to give away records; we once bought a hundred records at a penny a piece as a gag gift for a friend (a hundred of the same record!). Another source sold 45's for 10 cents each, so the market price varies. Xeroxing the invitation information and gluing it to old records makes a memorable invitation. Records also make wonderful decorations to hang around the party room, as well as great place mats for the table.

Try to locate some musical posters to hang around the house.

CHECKLIST

1. Send invitations
2. Start collecting items for instruments
3. Get records and music posters

3 STAGE THREE

1. Call your RSVPs.

2. Make one of each instrument with your child so you will be able to show the children what each is like (see pages 157–58).

3. Buy Ping-Pong balls for the relay race.

4. Collect the items you will need for playing the What Am I? game—guitar pick, violin bow, plastic string, drumstick, any vacuum cleaner attachment, cassette tape, typing ball from an IBM typewriter or a typewriter ribbon, inside metal ringer from a large bell, and the rubber part of a horn (used to squeeze the air to make a sound).

5. Make sure your tape recorder works, as you will want to tape the children's orchestra. If you have a video camera, get that ready, too.

6. If you know anyone who can play an instrument and knows how to do a sing-along, invite him to play at the party. This could be the same person you have chosen to lead the instrument-making and the festivities.

7. Make any final decisions about the menu. Our advice at this party is to make it very simple. Serve pizza from your local pizza parlor and concentrate on making a great birthday cake. Buy paper plates, cups and other disposables.

8. Gather together tapes of your child's favorite songs. You can use these for the games and for background music. A copy of *The Lone Ranger* theme (the *William Tell* Overture) would be great to use in the Ping-Pong Relay Race.

CHECKLIST

1. Call RSVPs
2. Make sample instruments
3. Get Ping-Pong balls
4. Collect things for "What Am I?" game
5. Check tape recorder
6. Invite a friend who can play and/or sing
7. Decide on menu; get accessories for table
8. Get tapes of songs

✳ To minimize the mess of cake serving, try this: Dorit and Vilma from The Pied Piper Toy Store in Manhasset, New York, suggest baking birthday cakes in flat-bottomed wafer ice cream cones (fill with batter from any cupcake recipe). Just add a scoop of ice cream, some sprinkles on top and stick a candle in the birthday child's cone.

STAGE FOUR

4

1. Bake the cake and refrigerate. Make the arrangements for pizza delivery.

2. Set the table with records, paper plates and cups (you can find these with record and/or music designs on them). If you have musical note stickers, paste them on the tablecloth.

Decorate with the posters and records.

3. Gather your music tapes and camera film so you won't have to look for them tomorrow.

4. Gather the items for making the instruments in one place in the party room. This will make it easier to organize the activities.

5. Get paper and pencils ready to play What Am I?

ACTIVITIES

These activities will work for ages four to twelve.

Have music playing as the children come in. Let them examine the instruments you have made as you wait for all the guests to arrive. If your "expert" is already there, have her play songs to keep the children occupied.

1. Making and Playing Instruments • Before you begin, have your "expert" sit the children around in a circle and talk to them about instruments and music. Ask her to be funny; this is not a classroom, but a party. Have them clap their hands and listen to the sound. Have them do it quietly, then loudly; slowly, then quickly. Now ask if anyone there can whistle. Let everyone try and listen to that sound. Have them put their hands on their hearts and see if they can hear the heart beat, like the sound of a drum.

Instructions for Making Instruments

1. Drums: Take the empty coffee cans, cover with the plastic lids and turn upside down. Let the child hit the drum with his hands, and then give him a plastic or wooden spoon to use as a drumstick.

2. Coffee Can Shakers: Fill empty coffee cans with beans and cover.

3. Soda Can Shakers: Empty any soda can and pull off the metal tab. Fill with 1 cup of uncooked rice. Tape the opening with packing tape.

> **CHECKLIST**
>
> 1. Bake cake and order pizza
> 2. Set table and decorate room
> 3. Gather tapes and records
> 4. Collect all items for making instruments
> 5. Prepare paper and pencils for What Am I? game

❋ Our friend Susan Strauss takes her six-year-old son Jonathan to concerts and ballets (he usually lasts through the intermission, but Susan figures that half a concert is better than none!). When it came time for his sixth birthday, Jonathan voted to have an Orchestra party. The Strausses hired Craig Woodson, a musician in Los Angeles who teaches children about instruments, to bring several instruments he designed with him. He taught the children how to make some, and then he organized an orchestra.

157

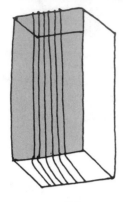

4. Milk Bottle Shaker: Take an empty plastic milk bottle and fill with 3 cups of uncooked popcorn. Close the opening with its bottle-cap and shake.

5. Kazoos: You buy these. Show the children how you can sing into the kazoo and make different melodies.

6. Cymbals: Give a child two metal pot lids and have her hit them together.

7. Graters: Take a plastic grater and rub a wooden spoon across it, going back and forth.

8. Shoebox Strummers: Take a couple of shoeboxes and remove the lids. Cut a 3-inch hole in the center of the lid. Pull six rubber bands lengthwise around the uncovered box and put the lid back on so that the rubber bands show through the hole. Tape the lid to the box, and you have a modified guitar.

9. Bells: You buy these in as many shapes and sizes as you like. They make wonderful and inexpensive instruments that you can give each child.

10. Glass Xylophone: Take six glasses and fill them with different amounts of water. Give the children metal spoons and have them play music on the "xylophone."

Now begin making the instruments listed above—you don't have to make them all. They are our suggestions, so make as many as you like, and add any you and your child want. Divide the children into the sections of the orchestra you are creating. Have a couple make the drums and play them in front of everyone. Now have two other children make the coffee can with beans. Then let them shake them. Continue making the other instruments and let the children hear their different sounds. Have them try each other's instruments. Let the different sections of your orchestra play together and listen to the different sounds. Direct them as a conductor would. Play soft, loud, slow, fast, and then try different rhythms.

You can now record the orchestra playing together. If you have a piano, have someone play a familiar song and let the orchestra accompany it. Play "Row, Row, Row Your Boat" (or any other song) slowly and then faster and faster.

2. Ping-Pong Relay • Not everything at this party has to be directly related to music, but it would be fun to play the theme from *The Lone Ranger* for this relay. Divide the children into two teams. The object is for the kids to blow a Ping-Pong ball back and forth, with their hands behind their backs, crawling on the floor. Each team has an even number of children on opposite sides of the room. The first child on Team 1 blows

TIP

Records make great invitations. Buy old, cheap 45 rpms. Trace the label and fill out with your party information. Xerox, cut out, paste over the old labels and send in padded envelopes.

the ball to her teammate across the room, who blows it back to another child on Team 1 on the other side of the room. When everyone on one team is done, that team wins.

3. What Am I? • The children are shown small objects which are part of larger objects all having to do with making sounds, musical or otherwise. You show them the "part" and they have to guess what it belongs to. Children from four to eight can guess out loud. Children aged eight to twelve write their answers down. Give each child a piece of paper and pencil. The one with all the correct answers wins.

4. LUNCH

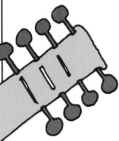

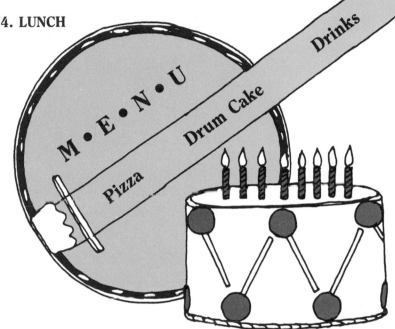

See the recipes on pages 230–31.

What Am I?

1. Guitar pick
2. Bow
3. Plastic String
4. Drumsticks
5. Vacuum Attachment
6. Cassette Tape
7. Typewriter Ball
8. Metal Ringer
9. Rubber Ball
10. Receiver

1. Guitar
2. Violin
3. Cello or Piano
4. Drum
5. Vacuum Cleaner
6. Tape Recorder
7. Typewriter
8. Bell
9. Horn
10. Telephone

ENTERTAINMENT

Appropriate and fun entertainment for this party is for someone to play an instrument and sing along with the children.

FAVORS

The instruments the children made go home with them. They also take home the kazoos and bells that you gave them. If you were able to get a lot of inexpensive records, you can include those in the favors package as well. You can also buy 45 rpm records—hits of the month—and give those to the older children.

ORIENTAL FESTIVAL

中原大國

Ages 5–12

[M] any children are fascinated by foreign cultures, and in this country, many such "foreign" societies are really not so foreign. Drive down the main street of many towns and you will see as many Oriental, Eastern European, Mexican and Far Eastern restaurants as you will fast-food hamburger hangouts. Many of today's children are familiar with popular "foreign" foods. What child hasn't bitten into a taco or an egg roll by the time she can recite the alphabet?

Parties with "imported" themes seem to be quite popular nowadays. As an example of this kind of party, we have created an Oriental Festival. Mexican Festivals, Russian Feasts or Hawaiian Luaus all have wonderful possibilities as well.

1 STAGE ONE

CHECKLIST

1. Plan general ideas for party
2. Make guest list and invitations
3. Start collecting decorations
4. Get items for games and activities

1. Start discussing the various parts of this party with your child. We assume you are having this party because your child has a particular affinity for things Oriental. Get her opinions, likes and dislikes, so you can plan the party of her dreams. Decide if you want this to be a costume party. Keep in mind that children love to dress up, and a costume party adds flavor and atmosphere to the festivities.

2. Make up your guest list and start making the invitations.

INVITATION

You can buy Chinese or Japanese fans at an Oriental store and write the copy for the invitations on the backs. Send them in padded envelopes. Even if you don't write Chinese, you might fake a few squiggles that look like Chinese characters on the backs of the envelopes (or you can ask someone at the Chinese shop to write out the letters for Happy Birthday in Chinese).

Another option for an invitation is to write it out on a piece of paper about 5 inches square, roll it around a pair of wooden chopsticks and fasten with a rubber band. Send it in the same envelope as described above.

Confucius Says:
COME HAVE FUN
AT
ANDREA'S
6TH BIRTHDAY
FESTIVAL AT
888 PERSHING SQUARE
Come in Oriental Dress
JANUARY 4TH AT 1:00 pm
R.S.V.P. 555-1234

3. Start collecting the decorations. At a Chinese market or gift store, buy the following inexpensive items: paper lanterns in different patterns, kites in various shapes, fans, bamboo sticks (you can get these at florists, too), lots of wooden chopsticks (at least triple the number of guests—some will be used for the invitations, some for the kites, others for eating, and still others for the decorations); miniature paper umbrellas (they make great decorations and will also go on the cupcakes), and plastic spoons and dishes. And if you're really into it, Chinese costumes for the parents (even straw hats and a cummerbund would have an effect!).

4. Get items for the games and activities. In an Oriental or American market buy the following: string, packages of LifeSavers rolls, crepe paper, balloons, Chinese items for the tray in Forget-Me-Not, magic markers, sequins and feathers, stickers and a whistle.

STAGE TWO 2

1. Call your RSVPs.

2. Set the menu. You can make the fortune cookies during these last two weeks, if you like. Get the other ingredients in one trip to an Oriental market.

3. There are a lot of activities at this festival. Go over the list and make sure you have all the things you will need. Practice making our chopsticks with your child (see Activity #7, on page 166). You may want to let him eat with them a couple of times before the party to give him a leg up on the other kids so he can be an expert at his party.

4. Start buying the favors (see page 167). A great way to wrap the favors is to put them in Chinese food containers, available from your local Oriental restaurant. Other popular containers for the favors are large woven plastic bags.

CHECKLIST

1. Call RSVPs
2. Set menu
3. Go over list of activities
4. Get favors

3 STAGE THREE

1. If you have not yet bought the food, do so now. Write the fortunes and bake the fortune cookies. You can also make the Umbrella Cupcakes the day before the party. Make the hard-boiled eggs not for eating, but for the Chinese Egg Roll game.

2. Set the table. If you can, hang lanterns over the table. Cover with an Oriental paper cloth and Oriental dishes. Put a pair of wooden chopsticks at every place setting (the children will make our version of Tweezer Chopsticks before they eat). Place fans in the center of the table. Whatever Chinese accessories you have, use them to decorate both the table and the party room to your heart's content.

3. Prepare everything for the games. Arrange the items for the kite-making activities on two tables (there are two kite-making activities—the kids will be making one kite to fly and one to hang on the wall). Put the items for the Forget-Me-Not on the tray and cover with a towel or scarf (you will also need paper and pencils). Prepare the strings for the LifeSavers. You will also need a lot of rubber bands and pieces of paper for making the Tweezer Chopsticks.

4. Prepare the favors you chose. Wrap them in individual Chinese food containers, write the child's name on the outside, close with a ribbon or sticker and set aside.

ACTIVITIES

1. Making Streamer Kites • The parents greet the guests at the door looking as Oriental as possible. As the kids arrive, lead them to a table full of kite-making materials. They will be making Streamer Kites, the kind you can actually wave around as if they were flying. Place the various colored crepe paper, the 12-inch chopsticks and the glue or double-face tape on the table. Cut the crepe paper into 6-foot lengths with the children, and show them how to tape one end to the chopstick and wave the other. The kids take these home.

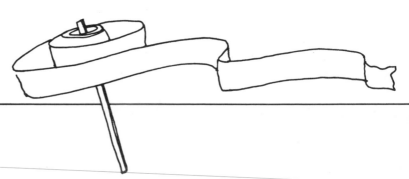

2. Forget-Me-Not • For this game, appropriate for ages eight to twelve, place items on a large tray. Let the children see them for 30 seconds. Then remove the tray and have them write down what they saw. Put at least as many items on the tray as there are children (when the game is over, you can give them out as favors). Give each child a paper and pencil so she can write down what she remembered.

Sample tray items: chopsticks, fan, fortune cookie, packet of soy sauce, paper umbrella, Chinese doll, miniature paper lantern, teacup, bell, miniature pagoda, bamboo basket, teapot or tea bag. You can use these items for prizes in the various activities.

* Mary Slawson returned from her trip to the Orient loaded with small, inexpensive gifts. They came in handy when her eight-year-old son Alexander picked a Chinese birthday party. His guests went home with bike bells, Chinese whistles, Chinese yo-yos and Chinese worker hats.

3. LifeSaver Race • Take the string or twine you kept wound up in a ball and cut two pieces about 3 feet long. Unwrap two packages of LifeSavers. Divide the guests into two teams. The object is to pass a LifeSaver on a string to your partner without using your hands. Two people from each team hold the string. One person puts one LifeSaver at the end of the string and maneuvers it, without her hands, from her end to her partner's. For a team to finish, each couple has to pass the LifeSaver. The team that finishes first wins a package of LifeSavers.

4. Kite Art • We call this "art" because the kids will want to hang these kites on their walls, not fly them in the wind. You need brown paper bags (the large kind, from the market), magic markers, stickers, sequins, feathers and lots of glue.

Give each child a paper bag to decorate to his heart's content. When he is done, help him tie strings to the four corners of the open end of the bag. Tie the four strings

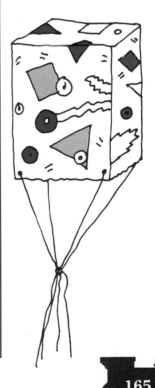

together about a foot from the bag and hang on the wall.

An alternative to this activity, especially if you made the simple streamer kites, is to invite an origami expert and have him teach the children this fine and fascinating Oriental art of paper folding.

5. Confucius Relay • Blow up two balloons. Divide the group into two teams and line them up in two straight lines, one child standing behind the other. Mark a starting gate at one end of the room and clear a path to the other end.

Give the first member of each team a pair of chopsticks and one balloon. Blow a whistle to start. The first player on each team rolls the balloon with the chopsticks towards the other end and back. Then he hands it, with the chopsticks, to the next person in line. Never touch the balloon with your hands! If the balloon gets away from you, you must retrieve it with the chopsticks. If it bursts, get another balloon.

6. Chinese Egg Roll • Use only hard-boiled eggs! Divide the group into two teams. The object is to roll an egg from one side of the room to the other with your nose. The first team to finish wins!

7. Making Chopsticks • You can have the children make Tweezer Chopsticks when they sit down at their Chinese Festival. While you are bringing the food, they will be making their "flatware." Give each child a pair of wooden chopsticks (the inexpensive kind that comes wrapped in paper). Don't throw the paper out—they'll need it! Wrap the end you hold with a rubber band as tightly as you can. Take the paper and fold it until it is about ½ inch long. Stick it between the chopsticks at the end with the rubber band. The result is tweezers that look like chopsticks and make even a two-year-old an impressive eater.

If you have traveled with your child, or if your family enjoys foreign experiences, why not choose a favorite country as your party theme? Use postcards as invitations, ethnic accessories as decorations and favors, play foreign games, and serve ethnic foods. Make sure this is your child's choice. For every Cara Ridgeway who loves sushi there is a Seth Familian who would rather devour tacos.

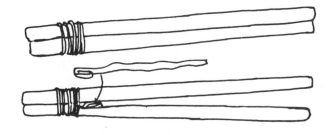

8. LUNCH

M • E • N • U
Chow Mein Noodles
Pineapple Barbecued
  Spareribs
Snow Peas
Madeline's Fortune
  Cookies
  Umbrella Cupcakes

See the recipes on pages 231–32.

FAVORS

Give out the favors after lunch. Straw hats (they cost very little at your local Chinese store), kites (they have made their own, or you can buy them), Chinese yo-yos and handcuffs, fans, ivory chopsticks, large Oriental bags or any other Oriental toys work well. The children may have won some of them at the games; others you have packed in the Chinese take-out cartons and/or plastic bags. Remember: Oriental goodies will be much appreciated by the kids.

✱ Bobbi Queen filled up small Chinese take-out cartons with little pencils, pads and stickers from an art supply store. She used press-on letters to "print" everyone's name on the outside.

PIRATE TREASURE HUNT PARTY

Ages 4 and up

What child hasn't dreamt of flying off to Never-Never Land and never growing up, or searching for pirate treasure with a golden sword in his hand and a patch on his eye? For the child whose dreams these are, and for those of us who never did grow up, what a treat to be able to travel into the world of Peter Pan and/or the Pirate's Kingdom.

Even the preparations for this party are fun. Once you and your child have decided to turn your house into Never-Never Land for a day, discuss the option of making this a costume party. You can ask the guests to come as pirates (this works for any age group) or to come as characters from Peter Pan (better for ages four to eight).

This party works either indoors or outdoors. In fact, we have designed it for both, but it is flexible enough so that you can hold it anywhere you like (and alter your plans according to the weather). If you have front and back yards, plan to use them, so if they need to be cleaned, this is the time to do it.

1 STAGE ONE

1. Prepare the invitation. Remember the stickers to decorate the envelopes; try getting those that would be appropriate for a pirate theme.

INVITATION

This invitation is to be written in invisible ink. You can do this on any invitation with a pirate image on it. Or you can xerox this invitation and write your own message inside.

The copy on the cover reads: "Secret Message Inside." On the inside write your message (e.g., "Beware! Brian is Having A Pirate's Party" or "Come Fly to Never-Never Land at Jonathan's Peter Pan Party" and then give the details: dress— as a Pirate, as a character from Peter Pan—time, date, place, RSVP, and any other instructions you may want to add). Be sure to add instructions in regular, visible ink that say: To read this message simply place it in front of a light bulb that is on and the message will magically appear.

You can use invisible ink made by Adam's Magic. Or you can dip a calligraphy pen in lemon juice and write the message with the juice.

2. Make your guest list and keep for RSVPs.

3. You will need a lot of "junk jewels" for this party, so start collecting now. You can start at the five-and-dime, thrift shops or bead stores for plastic jewelry and beads (large ones are best). Also ask around—you may be surprised by the number of friends who have attics full of old costume jewelry they would be glad to donate.

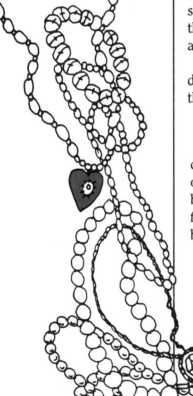

CUT ON FOLD OF PAPER

FOLD TO MAKE HAT INVITATION

STAGE TWO

1. Send invitations.

2. Decide on the decorations with your child: If you have a front yard, plan to turn it into a treasure world full of gold coins for the children to collect. Use bags of gold foil coins filled with chocolate or bubble gum (we suggest the gum only because the chocolate can melt and produce a mess). Buy bandannas, eye patches (you can get a bagful at party shops), gold rubber or plastic saber swords—and get some extras. Collect two or three corks to serve as charcoal make-up for pirate mustaches.

3. Buy inexpensive pirate hats to give out to each child as he walks in the door. If the children are already coming in costume, just use a few hats as decoration around the party room and on the table.

CHECKLIST

1. Send invitations
2. Prepare decorations
3. Get pirate hats

xxx *BEWARE!* xxx
BRIAN IS HAVING A
PIRATE PARTY
come dressed as a pirate!

TIME:_____ DATE:_____ PLACE:_____ RSVP:_____

TO READ THIS MESSAGE PLACE IN FRONT OF A LIGHT BULB

INSIDE

XXX

SECRET
MESSAGE
• INSIDE •

XXX   XXX

3 STAGE THREE

CHECKLIST

1. **Call any RSVPs**
2. **Collect decorations**
3. **Organize items for the games and activities**
4. **Buy several rolls of pennies at the bank**
5. **Collect records**
6. **Borrow an old-fashioned kitchen timer or alarm clock**
7. **Optional: Buy ID badges, one per guest**
8. **Optional: Get videotape**
9. **Get film and camera equipment ready**
10. **Set menu**

1. Call the RSVPs. Remind them about the costumes.

2. Collect the decorations; if there is anything else you need, this is the time to get it.

3. Organize the items you will need for your activities:

- For Blind Man's Bluff, draw a Treasure Map on large sheets of butcher or shelf paper. Get enough crayons in different colors so each child will have her own. Have a prize ready.
- For Captain Kidd's Treasure Hunt, collect small toys and gifts that the kids will get as prizes. Now cut out magazine photographs of these items (you hide the pictures; whichever picture they find, they keep that item). You can reverse the process by cutting out magazine photos and then buying those items. Roll each picture and tie with a pretty ribbon. Put them all in a carton until the day of the party.

Gather as many small cardboard gift boxes as there are children. Now collect different decorations that can be glued on the boxes—beads, sequins (better and cleaner than glitter), wrapping paper, lace, netting, yarn, plastic jewels, buttons, etc. Another great idea is to get gold stick-on letters (at a large stationery, art or architecture supply store) so the children can write their names on the boxes. Get lots of extras! The result of this effort will be the Treasure Chests for collecting their bounty and for holding the Treasure Hunt gifts.

4. Buy several rolls of pennies at the bank. Drop the pennies in a solution of 4 tablespoons salt and ½ cup vinegar to make them shine. Use this "gold" for prizes and to decorate the table.

5. Try to find the Disney record "It's a Small World" or "Pirates of the Caribbean" and/or the record of *Peter Pan*. These are for theme music and for Musical Chairs.

6. For Captain Hook's Crocodile Hunt, borrow a large, old-fashioned kitchen timer or alarm clock (digital just won't do!) that has a very loud ticking sound.

7. Buy ID badges (any metal buttons or badges will do: plain ones are better, but if you can't find those, buy any buttons because you'll end up covering them anyway). Now xerox the drawing on page 173, making one copy for each guest. On each "badge" write the child's name with a pirate-like introduc-

tion. Some examples are Long John Silver, Terrible Tom, Long-Toothed Larry, One-Legged Michael, Peter the Plunderer, etc. Cut out the circle that you copied and inscribed with the name and glue it on your badge. Repeat so that you have one badge per party guest.

8. If you're planning to have a very long party (our activities for this party should fill at least two hours, perhaps more), you can show a videotape of the movie *Peter Pan* or you can have a friend read a chapter or two from *Peter Pan* (this works well for younger kids up to the age of six).

9. Make sure you have enough film for your Polaroid-type camera. Giving each child a photograph of herself in this getup with her treasures in hand is a wonderful party favor.

10. Organize the menu:
  - get a cookie cutter in the shape of an X
  - make sure you have at least one Bundt cake pan (two would let you bake both cakes at once)
  - buy the apricot nectar, pineapple or orange juice, ginger ale or 7-Up, and orange or lemon sherbet for the Crocodile Brew

STAGE FOUR 4

1. Prepare the food; bake the cake and refrigerate.

2. Set the table. At this party, the table looks great covered with a black tablecloth. In the center, create a large mound of treasure made up of plastic jewels, toys, "gold money" (the gum coins wrapped in gold and/or the shiny pennies) and any other goodies you and your child have collected. Throw those gold coins everywhere on the table. Use as much of anything that is "gold." Gold wrapping paper or gold foil paper doilies make great place mats. Crinkling it up into small balls gives the table an added richness. If you can find gold-colored paper or plastic plates, use them. There are also a variety of paper goods available in pirate themes. Make that table look as much like an open, glittering treasure chest as you can.

CHECKLIST

1. Prepare food
2. Set table and decorate party room

5 STAGE FIVE

Not all parties have "that morning" plans, but this one has a couple of things you need to do.

1. Scatter lots of gold foil coins everywhere, especially in the front yard or entrance to your apartment. This will look wonderful as the guests arrive and will be a treasure they collect as they leave. Do the same thing on the carpet or in the front yard just before the kids leave (but not in the morning—the coins will never last).

2. Decorate the front door with a pirate's hat and an eye patch. Write "Come On In—If You Dare" or "Come Fly to Never-Never Land" or some such message on a banner and hang it over the front entrance. At the front door, have an umbrella stand full of gold plastic swords. Have a bowl of eye patches and bandannas.

3. Burn the ends of the corks. These will be used to draw mustaches on each arriving child. Assign this task to an adult or teenager. (This can be done days ahead.)

4. Set out the material for decorating the Treasure Hunt boxes on a large table so all the children can work there together. A table that is child's height and small child-size chairs (you can rent these at a party rental store) work best. If necessary, you can have the children sit on the floor.

5. Hide the Treasure Hunt magazine cut-outs that were rolled up a couple of weeks ago. Have the matching toys in a box ready to be distributed after the hunt.

ACTIVITIES

1. Blind Man's Bluff • Pin your Treasure Map up on a wall in the party room. Give each child a different color crayon. Using a bandanna, blindfold one child at a time, spin him around and point him towards the map. Let each child make a mark with his crayon on the Treasure Map. When everyone is done, the one who came closest to the treasure wins.

2. Treasure Chests • Sit the children around the table you prepared with the buttons, sequins, lace, glue, markers, wrapping paper, press-on letters, etc., on it. Hand them each a cardboard gift box and let them decorate to their heart's content. Encourage them to use their imagination. They can be fanciful, they can design around a theme, they can do anything they want! Have each child write his or her name on the chest. Don't make a contest out of this. Let the children have a great time, and keep reminding them that their Treasure Chests will soon be filled with the great treasures they will find!

3. Treasure Hunt • The version for five- to eight-year-olds is called the Picture Treasure Hunt. You have already hidden the magazine photographs of the treasures. Explain the game to the children. The object is to find as many "secret scrolls" as they can. The deal is this: they get to keep the object in that photograph. And off they go! If you are playing this indoors, play one of our suggested songs as they hunt. Urge them along as the hunt progresses and have other adults around to keep encouraging them.

Once all the children have returned, sit them down in a circle and hand out the Treasure Chests they made. Now let each in his turn unroll his "Treasure Scroll." Then encourage the "ooohs" and "aaahs" at his find while you reach into your treasure box and give him his matching gift. Continue until everyone has her treasures safely in her chest. Set the chests aside because there will be more to put in them later.

Another version of the Treasure Hunt that works with older kids is one we call Rhymer's Treasure Hunt. Write eighteen clues, each made up of a rhyming poem that asks the child to perform an act of some sort.

Examples:

Clue #1:
Roses are red
Violets are blue
The next clue you'll find,
Is under a shoe!

Clue #2:
(which is under a shoe)
Hop on one foot
To the very next clue
When you get to the front door,
It's right next to you!

Clue #3:
Now that you've found me,
Blink your eyes fast,
While you follow the steps,
To the one that is last.

Clue #4:
Hurry and skip,
Before it's too late,
To the nearest calendar,
With a circled date.
(circle the birth date and
write a clue in it)

This is a start—now go to it and make up the rest of the clues. You and your child will have as great a time writing the clues as the children will finding them.

＊ For Carol Schneider's son Eric's sixth bithday, Carol made a Treasure Hunt with simple clues which were questions describing obvious objects. Here's how they played: The children were divided into two teams—red and blue—and each team searched for the clues together. The first clue read: "You ring me to get into the house." The children ran to the doorbell, where they found the second clue: "I make pretty fires to keep people warm." The next one read, "I have lots of arms that reach up to the sky and I'm wearing a red belt" (the tree in the backyard had a red belt tied to its trunk). Just remember to remind the teams to leave the clues in place for others to find.

Note: There can be a problem with a Treasure Hunt. What if some kids find a lot of treasures and others none at all? You must be prepared for this possibility. There is inevitably one child who is more hesitant about going out to hunt, or slower to find the loot, just as there are always the more aggressive and courageous kids who find it all. Never let a child return from the hunt empty-handed. Scatter extra clues or put a limit on the number of treasures a child can find (you can issue a "Treasure Edict": as each child finds a certain number of treasures, he returns to the "Treasure Station" to await the others). This gives all the children a more even chance to participate successfully in the hunt.

4. Pirates of the Caribbean • Remember Musical Chairs? Of course we all do. You may think this is a tired old game, but if you ask your kids, we'll bet they just love it! In keeping with the Treasure Hunt theme, play any of the songs we mentioned earlier—"Pirates of the Caribbean," the theme from *Peter Pan* or any song your child just loves (you can always do "Happy Birthday").

5. Captain Hook's Crocodile Hunt • This is the time to get your loudest kitchen timer. Set it for anywhere from 3 to 5 minutes and hide it, telling only the birthday child where it is. Then have the children search for the clock by listening for the ticking. Remind them that only by being very quiet will they be able to hear the ticking sound (this is a great way to calm the children down after the tumult of the Treasure Hunt). As each child finds the clock, she is to tell only the birthday child where it is (this makes the birthday child feel very important!). The object is to have all the children find the clock before the alarm goes off.

You can repeat this game time after time.

6. Filling the Treasure Chests • This is not a game, but remember that the center of the table contains many toys for the children. When lunch is over, give them their Treasure Chest (it already contains the "finds" from the hunt) and help them fill the chest with the bounty from the center of the table: shiny pennies, plastic toys, "jewels," jelly beans and the like. Make sure each child gets some toys.

Teresa Nathanson, a mother of three boys, is an expert at this party. She has a great idea for dealing with children who have a difficult time competing with others. She keeps extra treasure pictures that she can hide at the last minute, and then guides the child who has not found anything towards that treasure.

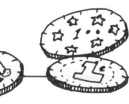

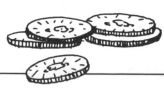

7. PIRATE'S LUNCH

M • E • N • U

Pirate Sandwiches
Captain's Salad
Crocodile Brew
Treasure Hunt Cake

See the recipes on pages 233–34.

ENTERTAINMENT

This is already a long, full party. If you wish to substitute a quieter activity for one or two of the games for the younger children, you can show a videotape of *Peter Pan* and/or read them the book. The older ones will be able to handle all the activities.

FAVORS

Give each child the Treasure Chest he made. Each is already filled with toys from the Treasure Hunt, plus goodies from the center of the table. Now make sure each child has his sword, eye patch and bandanna. As you lead them to the door, take a picture of each little pirate with his booty. As the final touch, let the children hunt for those gold coins in the front yard (or the front porch) on their way to the car. They may never leave!

✴ When Nora Ephron's son Jacob was eight, he went to a "city" version of the Treasure Hunt. Twenty guests were divided into four teams of five kids and one adult. Each team got a slip with questions and directions. Examples: "Go to 88th Street and Broadway. What three things are you not allowed to do there?" (Answers: smoking, loitering or spitting—all on the corner street sign.) Last direction: "Go to the northwest corner of 88th and Broadway and buy yourself a slice" (the adult had money for pizza for each team). Back at the house, everyone had ice cream and cake.

177

SAFARI

Ages 4–8

W hen Meredith's daughter Sarah was nearing her fifth birthday, the Brokaws were living in Washington, D.C. Sarah, the animal lover in the family, wanted to somehow include them in her birthday party. The Brokaws didn't think that a trip to the zoo would be particularly personal or unusual for Sarah. Meredith found that the local zoo had a trainer who came to people's homes to talk about the zoo animals he would bring. (Meredith didn't ask him which animals, which turned out to be a mistake.) Sarah suggested that the children come in costume, so they were invited to come dressed as their favorite animal. The invitations were sent—they were sponges in the shapes of animals, with paper invitations attached. And everyone waited for the magic day.

The children arrived—there was a bunny, cat, lion, raccoon, turtle and skunk. Sarah was the raccoon. Andy was the turtle (Sarah still remembers him as the cutest turtle she'd ever seen!), Katie was

the cat and Christa was the tiger. (How do we know? Sarah, who is now seventeen, still has vivid memories of this party that took place twelve years ago—which tells us something about the impression a wonderful party can have on a child!)

Everything was proceeding as planned until the trainer brought out the animals. Everyone loved the rabbit, and the puppy, and the beaver, and the parrot. But Christa the tiger did not like the boa constrictor, and she began to cry. Her fear threatened to turn what was a delightful party into a tearful nightmare.

Meredith quickly separated Christa from the others before they all started to cry. She put her in charge of watching the parrots in their cages in another room, and thereby prevented a catastrophic ending to the party. Now Sarah's memories of her Safari party are still joyful, so many years later, and Meredith remembers it as a lesson well learned: Not one party professional has crossed her doorway without Meredith knowing full well what was in store.

1 STAGE ONE

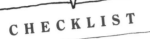

CHECKLIST

1. Locate an animal trainer and check out references
2. Decide on costume party
3. Prepare invitations

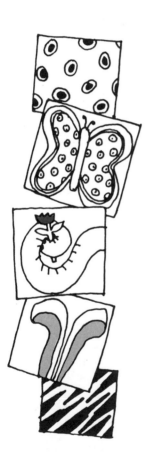

1. Call the local zoo, animal society or National Park Service, if there is one in your area, to find a well-qualified trainer who can bring several animals to the party and teach the children something about them. Be sure to discuss with him what animals he wants to bring. This is a party designed for four- to eight-year-olds. Keep in mind the personality of your own child. If he gets anxious at an animal he considers scary, make sure that animal doesn't come to visit. If your child has a favorite animal that might be appropriate (not a giraffe or tiger), ask the trainer to bring it. This is your child's party and you want it to be just right.

2. Decide whether or not you want a costume party. It really does add another delightful dimension to the party; you can ask that the children come as their favorite animal, or their favorite pet, or an animal they wish they could be, or a fantasy animal from their imagination.

3. Get that guest list together with your child. Make the invitations.

INVITATION

Children love puzzles. They love invitations, too. What could be better than a combination of the two?

You can draw your child's favorite animal or copy the one we have here (see page 181). Xerox as many invitations as you need, and then cut out the animal. Glue the cut-out on a piece of cardboard and have your child color in the animal on each invitation. Now cut each invitation into several large pieces, one at a time, and put the pieces in a padded envelope immediately (you don't want to get pieces from different invitations mixed up). Decorate each envelope with animal stickers, address and mail.

An alternative to the puzzle invitation is sending a capsule of an "instant grow" animal glued on the invitation. Be sure to include instructions for what to do with the sponge. This, too, can be placed in a padded envelope and decorated with animal stickers.

STAGE TWO

1. If you have not yet done so, send out the invitations.

2. Start helping your child plan his costume.

3. Buy plastic animals (for the Animal Hunt and to top the cake); badges and ribbons for prizes; copy our Match-Up game; bug boxes, butterfly nets, camouflage fabric and white netting (you can also use mosquito netting, which you can find at camping supply stores, or ordinary cheesecloth). You can buy inexpenisve "Zoos"—a collection of various plastic animals that come in a small bag and are great for prizes. Buy or make ribbons for prizes.

4. If you have decided against a costume party, you can get inexpensive safari or straw hats for each child.

5. Borrow from a friend and/or buy an Animal Lotto game at your local toy store (you will need an extra one as a prize).

C H E C K L I S T

1. Send out invitations
2. Plan costume
3. Buy animal accessories
4. Buy hats
5. Get Animal Lotto, ribbons and other prizes

3 STAGE THREE

1. Call anyone who has not responded.

2. Decide on your menu. Buy or borrow cookie cutters in the shape of animals for the sandwiches. Buy animal crackers for the cake (get several boxes—you can count on at least half the cookies being broken).

3. Start thinking about your decor. You have camouflage and netting fabrics. Discuss with your child different ways of wrapping the party room. Gather your houseplants in the entry hall or party room (you can also borrow some of your neighbors' plants) to give the room the feeling of a jungle. If you are having lunch outside, you may want to drape the trees with netting or camouflage fabric, put up a tent in which you can have lunch, or use the fabric as the tablecloth on a picnic table.

4. Xerox our Safari Match-Up game, making enough copies for all the children. Be sure you have pencils for everyone, too.

5. Collect magazines with your child, particularly any that are nature-related. Choose as many pictures of animals as you have guests. Now cut out the pictures, and then cut out the parts of the animals—noses, ears, heads, bodies, trunks, etc. These will then be glued together at the party.

STAGE FOUR 4

1. Decorate the party room or rooms. Now is the time to use those fabrics to cover up as many pieces of furniture or walls as possible. Drape the dining room table with camouflage fabric. Hang mosquito netting over the table to create a tentlike effect, fastening it to the ceiling with strong tape. Have your child collect all her stuffed animals and place them around the party room. Cluster plants to give the feeling of a jungle.

2. Buy coconuts and bunches of bananas. Use them on the table, and hang them at the front door or anywhere else they will add to the atmosphere you are creating.

3. Set the table. You have draped it with the fabric. You may have already placed bananas and coconuts as part of the centerpiece; now add assorted plastic animals at each place setting. Use paper plates and cups. If you have a yard, get some large leaves and fasten them around soda cans with rubber bands.

4. Bake the Safari Chocolate Cake.

5. Put the favors together. If you are planning the Bug Hunt, the children can take their bug boxes home. If not, make them part of the favors. The same goes for the hats (if the children are in costume, you may save the hats as favors). You can also give out boxes of animal crackers and any paperback books about zoos or animals. (See the section on Favors, page 185.)

ACTIVITIES

1. Animal Cut-Outs • As the children arrive, have them begin this activity. Take the cut-outs of animals that you set aside a couple of weeks ago. Lay out the different parts on a table and give the children colored construction paper and glue. Let them create their own animals from the cut-outs. The result will be hilarious—and they will have an extra prize to take home.

2. Costume Prizes • Give the children prizes for their costumes. Be sure to give each child a ribbon. Some awards might be for best four-legged animal, best two-legged animal, tallest animal, best animal that crawls, most original animal, the softest animal.

CHECKLIST
1. Decorate room
2. Buy coconuts and bananas
3. Set table
4. Bake cake
5. Prepare favors

3. Animal Trainer and Brood • Now that the children feel more at home and are already happy with their unexpected prizes, the animal trainer can begin. First he will show the children the animals he has brought, then talk about them and let the children pet at least one or two. Encourage the children to ask questions. Be sure to make them feel comfortable—this is supposed to be fun! If any children seem to be unhappy, anxious or fearful, and you are unable to soothe them easily, separate them from the crowd. Put them in charge of getting one of the other games ready so they will feel useful and not left out. It is not unusual for young children to have some fears, so try to make sure that a child who is afraid of animals doesn't feel silly or different. Anyway, this is neither the time nor the place to try to convince a child that "there is nothing to be afraid of."

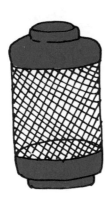

4. Animal Lotto • This is the perfect quiet game to follow the animal show. Just follow the rules on the box. The one to win gets a prize—her own Lotto game.

5. Animal Hunt • Children love to hunt for anything, so the plastic animals hidden in the jungle you have created in your party room are perfect. While the children are playing Lotto, have another adult hide the plastic animals everywhere (you can do this the day before, but you risk a very curious and clever birthday child finding them). The rule is: finders, keepers! Always have extra animals on hand to hide in case some children have been unable to find any animals.

6. Safari Match-Up • For children who can read, give each one paper with the Match-Up game and a pencil. The first child to get them all wins a stuffed animal or a Zoo set.

TIP

Make sure the trainer has done this in front of children before. Ask him for the names of people he has entertained and don't be shy about talking to them. It is always a good idea to "preview" any outside entertainment by talking to those who have used it.

SAMPLE MATCH-UP:

LION	CONSTRICTOR
GAME	ZEBRA
HUGE	AFRICA
TALL	JEEP
BOA	HUNTER
STRIPED	GAZELLE
SNOUT	RHINOCEROS
KENYA	ELEPHANT
FAST	GIRAFFE
DRIVE	KING

7. Bug (or Butterfly) Hunt • If you have extra time, or if you prefer that the children spend more time outdoors rather than play the other games, have them go on a Bug or Butterfly Hunt. Since this is usually a difficult task, it will keep them busy for a while. The Bug Hunt especially is a lot of fun. Just give them their bug box and off they'll go.

8. SAFARI LUNCH

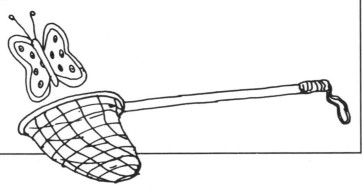

M • E • N • U

Animal Sandwiches
Celery Sticks
Safari Chocolate Cake
Drinks in Cans

See the recipes on page 235.

FAVORS

Your little animal guests will go home with pictures of themselves in their adorable costumes, with their safari hats (if this was not a costume party), bug boxes, drawings and animal cracker cookies. You can also add any paperback book about animals.

✳ When Geraldine Stutz gave a birthday party for her nephew Michael, she asked each mother to send a picture of her child. Gerri then had each photo blown up and glued one on each party favor box. At the party she formed a pyramid with the pictures facing the entry. The kids were absolutely delighted when each walked in and saw his or her own picture! And they had no trouble finding their favors when the party was over.

185

SPACE
FANTASY

Ages 4–12

K ids have been dreaming about entering the galaxy since long before Neil Armstrong stepped on the moon. Rocket ships, space monsters and astronauts are part of our children's lives and of their fantasies. For that child who dreams of outer space, who yearns to fly, who talks of shooting stars and draws moon rocks and can name the planets at the drop of an astronaut's helmet, this is his party.

From the minute the guests arrive in their space getup, to their wide-eyed wonder at the galactic atmosphere you've created, to their delight at playing super space games, to their wonder and pleasure at eating astronaut's treats—the success of this party is assured.

1 STAGE ONE

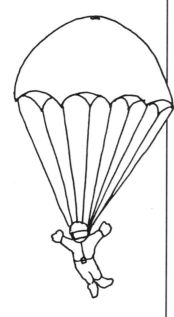

1. Do you want this to be a costume party? Having the children arrive dressed in astronauts' costumes or their version of space monsters does add an extra touch to the party.

2. Go over the games planned for this party (there should be more games than you need). Choose from among these activities (you may want to prepare for them all just in case). Start making a shopping list of things to buy and borrow in the weeks to come.

3. Go over the menu with your child. For the Crater Cake, you can order wonderful astronauts from Wilton Enterprises, Inc., 2240 West 75th Street, Woodridge, IL 60517. (Wilton guarantees your order will arrive within ten days, but just to make sure, order it now.) The Spaceship Topper Set has a silver spaceship plus spacemen and astronauts and is perfect for your Crater Cake. No. 2111-P-2008, approx. $3.69 for the set.

4. If you choose the favors we have listed, please note that some must be ordered or bought ahead of time.

5. Discuss the invitation, make it now and mail.

INVITATION

Copy (xerox) the drawing on page 189, fill out the information and attach the rocket ship to a freeze-dried Astronaut Ice Cream packet (available in toy stores or backpacking supply stores). Or you can cut out Mylar stars and string them to the invitation. Write in your information and send in a padded envelope. Have your child write the following on the envelope with silver or gold permanent markers: "Enter the Space Galaxy."

2 STAGE TWO

1. If you haven't yet done so, send out the invitations. Make up your RSVP guest list.

2. Buy or borrow the following items for your games and favors (at any toy stores): Leon Neon, Lite Ups (strings, balls, rods), Black Light streamers, one or two Volcano Kits (you must make the volcanoes ahead of time); small metal silver buckets (you can buy them at any garden supply store); lots of paper clips, magnets and string for the Moon Rock Search; dry ice (you can find it in your local yellow pages under "Ice Dealers." It is sold by the pound. Approximate price is 60 cents a pound, or ten pounds for $6.00); rocks and silver paint for place cards; cassette tape from the movie *2001* or *Star Wars* for Comet Dance and Shooting Star; balloons, plastic straws, string and masking tape for the Rocket Races; Wiffle golf balls, plastic golf clubs and coffee cans for Crater Golf; a 24-foot parachute (available to buy or rent at a gymnastics supply store). Buy some blue light bulbs.

3. A great prop for a Space party is colored eyeglasses so the children can see everything in different colors. You can make the eyeglasses out of cardboard (see page 191) and send them with the invitation (instructing the guests to bring them to the party) or you and your child can make them and hand them out at the party.

3

CHECKLIST

1. Call RSVPs
2. Set menu

4

CHECKLIST

1. Bake cake
2. Set table and decorate
3. Gather space toys
4. Install colored light bulbs
5. Get out the dry ice
6. Prepare favors
7. Make sure items for games are ready

STAGE THREE

1. Call any people who have not responded.

2. For our menu you will need: Astronaut Ice Cream packets, Shakely Voyageur Shakes (they come two to a pack) and Astronaut Strawberries (dehydrated), which you can serve with our lunch or give them out as favors; an extra-long submarine sandwich (you can make one or order one at a sandwich store or deli); Tang drink mix; ingredients for the Crater (Bundt) Cake.

STAGE FOUR

1. Bake the cake. Pick up or make the Rocket Sandwich (unless your party is in the afternoon, in which case you can take care of the sandwich in the morning). Get a metal funnel ready.

2. Set the table. Cover the entire table with aluminum foil. Scrunch it up a little in your hands, then spread on the table to cover completely. Use paper plates, cups, plastic spoons in silver, black or brown to accentuate the space or moon feeling. Leave a space for the volcanoes which will go in the center of the table (you will light them at lunch). For place cards, have your child spray-paint the rocks you collected silver. When they dry, write each child's name on a "moon rock" (you can use tube paint) and set at each plate.

3. Gather any rocket ships or spaceships your child owns and spread them around the party room and/or the table.

4. Make the party room a darkened space. Change the light bulbs to blue whenever possible. Hang the black light strips around the room.

5. If you bought dry ice, plan to put it outside the front door (or in your hallway or party room) just before the kids arrive tomorrow. You can put it in a silver garbage can. The effect of dry ice smoking is really fabulous!

6. Get your favors ready. Place them in the metal silver buckets and set aside.

7. Prepare the games. Get out all the things you'll need and make the accessories like the Robot Arms—magnets tied to long strings—today.

ACTIVITIES

If you are using colored glasses, hand them to each child as she enters the door. Having the children walk around looking at everything through the colored lenses will keep them occupied until everyone arrives. If you want to give prizes for costumes, you can do that when the children arrive as well.

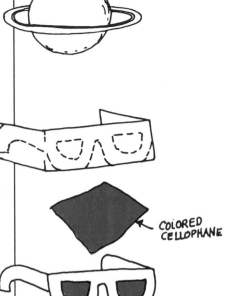

COLORED CELLOPHANE

1. Shooting Star • You will need the Fun Ball made by Lite Up (buy extra refills). Activate the ball when the party begins (it will stay lit up for about two hours). Sit the children in a circle in the darkened "Space Room." Play the *2001* or *Star Wars* theme. While the music is playing, the ball is passed from child to child. When the music stops, whoever has the ball is out of the game. One of these balls would make a good prize.

2. Moon Rock Search • Set up the game in the morning. Make a barrier (you can turn a table on its side) and cover with silver lamé fabric or aluminum foil. Behind the barrier place a laundry barrel or basket full of paper clips. When ready to play, give each child a Robot Arm and let him fish for "moon gems" (the paper clips). The child who gets the most wins. (You may want to have one of your helpers stationed behind the barrier to help any stray clips get on the magnets.)

3. Comet Dance • Give each child an activated Lite Stick. Darken the room. Play one of your musical choices. When the music stops, everyone has to freeze. Whoever moves is out of the game. Encourage the children to wave their Lite Sticks. Take pictures while the children are dancing (you will need fast film for this)—the results will be hysterical.

4. Parachute Fun • This game, for which you will need a backyard or giant playroom, is a great favorite of children everywhere. Let the children hold the round parachute at the edges. Practice having them raise and lower their arms so the parachute floats and billows in the air. Now play some variations: (a) You can have the birthday child under the parachute while it goes up and down. When he tags someone, that child joins him under the parachute; (b) You can assign numbers to the children. When a number is called, that child gets to run under the parachute. You can call two numbers and have one catch the other; (c) Another version is to have one child go under the parachute and another on it. Have them crawl around trying to catch one another.

5. Rocket Races • The day before the party, cut two 17-foot lengths of string. To play, divide the party into teams of two (the number of chairs will depend on your number of guests). Line up sets of two chairs approximately 15 feet apart. Each team will tie one end of the string to the back of one chair and push the loose end through a straw. Now they will tie the other end to the opposite chair back. Next, each team blows up a balloon and tapes it to the straw. (Put tape around the filled balloon and the straw, but don't tape the opening of the balloon.) After everyone has taped his balloon to the straw and is still pinching the balloon shut so that it can't release the air, everyone should let go at the same time and see which balloon reaches the other side first. This is both an outdoor and indoor activity.

6. Crater Golf • While you are playing one of the other games, have a helper set up the Crater Golf Course. Use empty coffee cans with both ends open and place them at various spots around the room. You can add a dog dish or a practice putting dish here and there. Give each child a plastic golf club and a Wiffle golf ball. Assign each child a number (the first number goes first). Now have them do the course; the first to finish wins. You may want to try playing the game with your child a few days before the party. It is a lot of fun and it will familiarize him with how you play.

7. Scrambled Planets • This is best for ages eight to twelve. Give the children the list of scrambled planets (left). They have a certain amount of time to unscramble the names.

1. UTIPREJ	JUPITER
2. NUSRAU	URANUS
3. TEENUNP	NEPTUNE
4. UANRTS	SATURN
5. RHEAT	EARTH
6. ONOM	MOON
7. SNU	SUN
8. SRMA	MARS
9. UPTOL	PLUTO

A creative customer of Carol Chalmer's Toy Store in Sun Valley, Idaho, made a spaceship cake decorated with lots of Legos and a Lego spaceship. Helium-filled Mylar balloons added to the "heavenly bodies" atmosphere. They come in shapes of stars and moons. Remember, helium lasts, so you can have them blown up the day before.

8. SPACE LUNCH

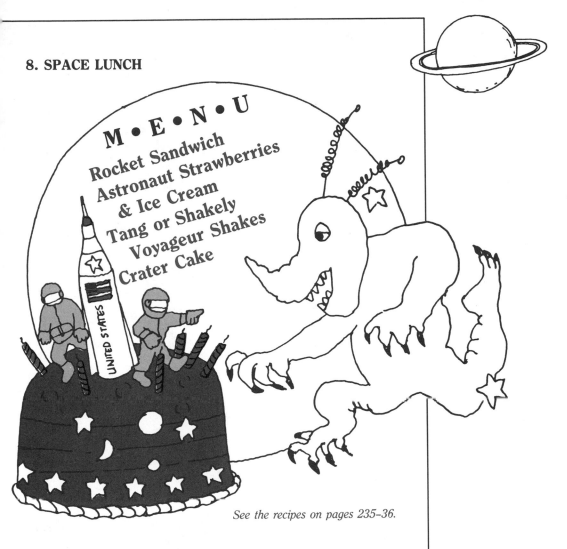

M • E • N • U
Rocket Sandwich
Astronaut Strawberries
& Ice Cream
Tang or Shakely
Voyageur Shakes
Crater Cake

See the recipes on pages 235–36.

ENTERTAINMENT

If you want some entertainment as well or instead of any of the games you might ask a high school student, preferably a science whiz, to come and perform some experiments.

FAVORS

The metal pail full of Fun Balls, Lite Up Sticks, magic rocks, plastic astronaut figures, marbles or any small toys is a great favor. If you did not use the Astronaut foods with your menu, give them as favors. Depending on the age, star maps make great favors.

✳ David and Jean Halberstam's five-year-old daughter Julia loved her Mom's way of giving out favors. Jean wrapped a big box with a removable top and filled it with little favors, individually wrapped, that were attached to different-colored ribbons. All the ribbons came out of the box top and ended at each child's plate. As ice cream and cake were served, the children pulled out their favors and unwrapped them.

Ages 3–5

H ave you ever met a child who, when asked, "Do you want to go anywhere?" couldn't be packed and ready before you finish your question? Children love taking trips. They love the suitcases, the buses and airplanes, the restaurants, the new people and sights. In short, they love the idea of traveling anywhere.

If your child is such a trip-taker or trip-dreamer, suggest this party. It's easy to plan, a lot of fun, and is even educational (but don't breathe a word of this to anyone!).

1 STAGE ONE

1. You and your child must choose a country to visit. This can be a place you have traveled to, one you have talked about or one that has a special fascination for your child. The party we loved was given by Paul and Maggie Moss Tucker for their son Jonathan, who is crazy about England.

2. Make up your guest list. If you are inviting older children, think of jobs you can assign them. Recruit some adults to be flight attendants, tour guides, interpreters, etc.

3. Make and send the invitations.

CHECKLIST

1. Choose a country with your child
2. Make up guest list
3. Make and send invitations
4. Plan decorations and costumes
5. Invite a "native" friend

INVITATION

Use a blank airline ticket and fill it out with the necessary information. You can also use picture postcards from the country you will be visiting.

JOIN US!

IT'S
JONATHAN'S BIRTHDAY
and We're Taking a Trip to London

TAKE OFF: Sunday, March 4TH
12:00 P.M.
FROM: 666 Sonoma Lane
RETURN: 2:00 P.M.

confirm reservations at 555-1234.

4. Start planning the decorations and costumes. The kids can color the flag of the country they will be visiting (we'll make the Union Jack). Dress yourself and your husband as an airplane pilot and a flight attendant. Any accessory like a pilot's hat, wings' pin or headset will help set the stage.

If there are "native" accessories, collect them. For England hang up the Union Jack, pictures and/or posters of the Tower of London, London Bridge, the Queen of England, etc.

5. If you know someone from England (or your chosen country), invite him to be the "star" whom you will visit on this trip or the "tour guide." Jonathan's dad's friend, a professor from England, was delighted to come act as the guide. If your friend can wear a costume (even a bowler and umbrella is simple and effective) you'll be ready to go!

STAGE TWO

1. Call the RSVPs. You can ask the guests if they have any indigenous costumes, and if they do, have them bring them. The more you can add to the atmosphere, the better.

2. One part of the party room will be turned into an "airplane." You can simply line up chairs in two rows with an aisle between them and pretend this is an airplane. If you like, you can have the children sit on the floor in two rows. Children have wonderful imaginations and don't need too much fuss to have a great time!

You will need two "thrones" for the presentation of gifts to the birthday "king." Simply get two old chairs (the bigger and stuffier, the better) and drape with any fabric. Buy or make two crowns and you're set.

3. Plan the menu. We will be having a picnic at Hyde Park so the meal is simple. Pack each lunch in a red or blue lunch box which can then be a party favor. If lunch pails aren't your choice for favors, just brown bag each lunch. Our menu calls for tiny "tea" sandwiches (you can cut them with an airplane cookie cutter), juice and cupcakes.

4. Decide on the favors and start buying or making them now. (See what is available in your area.) Your guests will have the flag they make and their lunch box. In addition you can give out English bobby hats. Another option is to buy briefcase-size cardboard boxes with handles; these "luggage" pieces are fun to carry on the airplane!

5. Prepare the items for your activities.

- You will need the outline of the British flag on pieces of paper for the kids to color (be sure to get red, white and blue crayons). If you buy 18-inch dowels for each guest, you can tape the flags onto them.
- Consult with your English friend to make a list of words the kids may not know.
- Collect slides to show on the "tour." If you don't have your own, don't panic. Call your local library. Chances are it has slides you can borrow.
- Make a drawing of Big Ben and cut out paper hands for the clock.
- Get the strings for Jump the River Thames.
- Make "Passports" for all the travelers.

CHECKLIST
1. Call RSVPs
2. Plan decorations
3. Plan menu
4. Decide on favors
5. Buy items for games and activities

✳ When Maggie Moss Tucker was ten, she went to a friend's party at her dad's advertising office. The children sat in the conference room and held a "meeting." The father explained how advertising works and gave the children an assignment: to come up with a new campaign for their favorite cereal and soda. They used the copying machines, typewriters and general office equipment.

3 STAGE THREE

1. Collect all the items for your activities. If you have arranged to check out slides from the library, do it today. Put all the things you will need for the games in one place.

2. Make sure you have everything you need for the costumes.

3. Get the wooden crate for the Speaker's Corner. If you need any other decorations, gather them today. Put them up in the party room, set up the airplane and the thrones.

4. Don't forget the camera equipment. There will be moments at this party you won't want to miss!

ACTIVITIES

As the children arrive, they are met by the pilot and/or flight attendant. Your child can hand each guest his passport and "suitcase," if you have them.

1. Flag Making • It works well to have everyone begin coloring their flag immediately while you are waiting for all the guests to arrive. When the children are done, put their names on the flags and fix them to the dowels. Have them bring their flag, passport and suitcase (if they have one) and get ready to board the airplane. The pilot or flight attendant now recites a few airplane regulations (buckle seat belts, no smoking, etc.). He describes the long trip, talks about flying, etc.

2. Learning British • Seat the children in the airplane in a regular airplane seat formation (the floor is fine). Introduce them to their "Tour Guide," your English friend. Have him teach the children "English" (bonnet, nappy, mackintosh, bobby, lorry, tuppence, etc.) so they will be ready to speak the language when they get there.

3. Taking the Trip • Pretend the airplane is taking off. Have the children buckle their seat belts. Have the pilot talk about airplanes and flying over the ocean.

4. First Day in London • The plane lands and the children go through "Customs" (have them show their passport and open their suitcase). Now they are ready to board their "Double Decker Bus." Once they are seated they are greeted by the "Tour Guide," who shows them the slide show of the sights of London. Make believe they are actually visiting each of these famous places as the slides come up on the wall. The first picture they should see is of their Double Decker Bus.

CHECKLIST

1. Make final preparations for activities
2. Prepare costumes
3. Get wooden crate
4. Get cameras

SPEAKER'S BOX

M • E • N • U

Airplane Sandwiches
Apple Juice
Lemon Kiss
Cupcakes

5. LUNCH IN HYDE PARK

See the recipes on page 236.

The tour ends at "Hyde Park." (If the weather permits and you have a backyard you can actually have this picnic outside.) Place the wooden crate you prepared at one end and explain to the children about Speaker's Corner. While the children are eating their lunch out of their lunch box, each can take a turn at the Speaker's Box, talking about whatever she wants.

When lunch is done, have the children form a Flag Parade, to march around the "park" waving the flags they have made.

6. Presentation of Gifts • After lunch you can have the ceremony of the "Presentation of Gifts to the Birthday King (or Queen)." Bring the kids to the thrones. Have the birthday child put on his crown and sit on the King's throne, where he will receive the gifts. The other children take turns sitting in the second throne as they present their gifts. The children love this ceremony, and it quiets them down from the trip's excitement.

7. Jump the River Thames • Place two lengths of 6- to 8-foot string on the ground, parallel to each other. Start with them about a foot apart. The river is the long space between the two strings. The kids take turns jumping over the river (it gets wider as the adults part the strings).

8. Big Ben • The "English" version of Pin the Tail on the Donkey is simple. Tape the drawing of Big Ben you and your child made on the wall. Blindfold each child and give her the hands of the clock, then let her try to attach them to the drawing with masking tape.

9. Return Trip Home • Load the plane for the trip back to the U.S. During the plane ride you can read *Madeline in London, Paddington Bear Goes to London* or *This Is London* to the children. This is a good "quiet" activity as they return "home" and their parents pick them up.

FAVORS

Your little guests will be taking home some or all of the following: passports, flags, suitcases, lunch boxes, bobby hats or other British memorabilia.

If a game isn't working, don't try too hard. Cut it short and move right on to the next one.

✳ Eppie Lederer, also known as Ann Landers, took her daughter Margo on a birthday cruise, when she was twelve, so they could spend time alone together. On her birthday, Margo was invited to sit at the Captain's table, where she received a special gift—she was permitted to play a song on the piano. She played "Deep Purple" and received wild applause. Little did the audience know that this was the only song she could play!

WESTERN ROUND-UP PARTY

Ages 4–12

C hildren love cowboys. At one time or another in their lives, children dream of riding horses, roping cattle, cheering at rodeos and holding their breath at the shoot-out at the neighborhood corral. Most of us may not get many chances to rope cattle, ride into the sunset or even cheer that brave guy who manages to stay on that steer longer than we thought possible. But we can pretend by having our very own western round-up. So for the young cowboy or cowgirl in your home—the one who ropes your pillows and rides your brooms and every now and then shoots at your refrigerator and asks for dinner under the stars—here's a party to remember.

Your backyard or the park is a natural setting for this party. There's nothing like a real campfire to make each guest feel like an authentic cowboy. But there's nothing to prevent you from being western indoors. The imagination of a child can complete any scenario that you begin.

1 STAGE ONE

CHECKLIST

1. Make up guest list
2. Make and send invitations
3. Collect decorations and equipment
4. Prepare games

1. Make up your guest list. This party can be adapted for kids ages four to twelve. For four- and five-year-olds, eliminate the Scavenger Hunt and keep the party to two hours. Older children can handle all the activities.

2. Make and send the invitations.

INVITATION

Tie pieces of heavy twine into knots. Then glue the knots to a written invitation. Place in a brown paper sandwich bag and mail in a brown envelope. You can substitute a lariat for the knot. Or you may prefer to write the invitation with a black magic marker on a brown sandwich bag. Fold this bag and mail in an envelope. It will have a rustic feeling.

COME ROPE SOME FUN
AT JOHN'S WESTERN ROUND-UP
Dress As A Cowboy or Cowgirl!
SATURDAY, OCTOBER 12 1-3 PM
AT 44 CLIMATE DRIVE
RSVP 555-1234

3. Start collecting the decorations. You will need cowboy hats; sheriff's badges; lots of red bandannas (you can hand these out to the arrivals at the front door and also use them as table or picnic decorations); plastic toy horses and any other cowboy toys your child has around the house (for the center of the table); weeds (also for atmosphere on the table).

If you are having the picnic outdoors, you need minimal equipment—a blanket or two, tables for serving and preparing the food, any materials for a campfire. If you are having the picnic indoors, you can go so far as to rent Astroturf (grass) at a party rental store and have the picnic on it.

Serve the lunch on metal pie tins at either picnic. You can buy disposable tins at any market.

4. Prepare game materials. You will need:

- A large plastic wading pool and some sand for Panning for Gold (great fun for younger ages), rolls of pennies, and plastic or metal strainers (the kind children use for sand play are perfect, as are ordinary kitchen strainers). If you play this game indoors you will merely need to hide the pennies around the house. If your penny hunt is indoors, use the strainers or paper bags to hold the pennies. Shiny pennies will seem more like "gold," so if there is time, have your child get them ready by giving them a vinegar and salt bath (see the Magic party, page 132).
- A Velcro dart board
- Lists of the items for the Scavenger Hunt to be xeroxed for the individual teams. You will also need brown paper shopping bags.

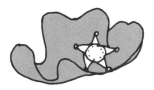

STAGE TWO 2

1. Call the RSVPs. Remind the guests about coming dressed in costume.

2. Go over the menu. It is our version of a typical western picnic. You can prepare most foods ahead of time, except the hot dogs, which have to be grilled or boiled just before lunch. You can substitute Sloppy Joes for the hot dogs, if you like.

3. Prepare the favors. Books on cowboys or knot tying are great. Lanyards, lariats, sets of plastic cowboys and horses, and toy stagecoaches all work well. You will also be giving out the red bandannas and/or cowboy hats.

CHECKLIST

1. Call RSVPs
2. Go over menu
3. Prepare favors
4. Prepare music and locate a musician recruit
5. Prepare the Scavenger Hunt list and recruit neighbors
6. Get help
7. Make Scavenger Bags
8. Buy rope

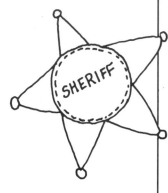

4. Prepare the music. You might find records of cowboy songs your child is familiar with—"I've Been Working on the Railroad," "On Top of Old Smokey," "Ragtime Cowboy Joe" and more. Write down the lyrics, xerox them and give them out to the children for the sing-along. If you know anyone who can play a guitar, recruit him for the children's sing-along. If not, use the records as the accompaniment, or just sing a cappella. No one is auditioning for the Met—"real" cowboys must sometimes have sung off-key.

5. Prepare the scavenger list and xerox. Plan to mark the places the children can visit with balloons or cowboy hats. Make maps detailing the scope of the hunt so the kids will have guidelines.

6. Get that help you will need. Both for serving the picnic, handling the activities and particularly for helping with the Scavenger Hunt, you will need additional adult supervision. Arrange for it now.

7. You and your child can now make the Scavenger Hunt bags. Take brown paper shopping bags and have your child personalize each by writing a team's name on each bag (the names should be cowboy-related: Big Bad John. Wyatt Earp, Long John Silver, Tonto, etc.).

You can make similar bags for the favors. Use brown paper lunch bags, label with the children's names and fill with the favors. These will also be used to hold the pennies that the children will find.

8. Buy pieces of rope for the knot-tying activity.

Polly Merrill's Scavenger Hunts always include one item that is impossible to find, like a 3-footed monster, a turkey buzzard, etc. Everybody uses his imagination to make a facsimile.

3 STAGE THREE

1. Make the food and bake the cake. Have all the prepared dishes ready to serve, the condiments in serving plates, and the hot dogs and buns ready to be cooked.

2. Decorate today. If the picnic is outside, prepare the area. If it is indoors, have the blankets or Astroturf ready. Have lots of napkins and extra cups. Get those pie tins ready.

3. Prepare the games. Fill the wading pool with sand and put the pennies in it. If your penny hunt is indoors, you can hide the pennies today. Gather the strainers. The Scavenger

CHECKLIST

1. Make food and bake cake
2. Decorate
3. Prepare games
4. Call neighbors

Hunt should be all ready. Check to make sure you have enough copies of the list and enough adults to supervise.

4. Call your neighbors who are participating in the Scavenger Hunt. Remind them that the hunt is tomorrow. You can mark their doors today with balloons or cowboy hats.

ACTIVITIES

If the guests have not dressed up in western attire, you will have them "in character" immediately by giving each one a bandanna to tie around his neck, a sheriff's badge or a cowboy hat as he arrives.

1. Knot Tying • For the first activity, as the children are trailing in, give them ropes so they can start practicing tying the knots. By the time everyone has arrived, they will have each tied some knots and be ready to go on to the next activity.

2. Panning for Gold • Give two children strainers and have them pan for as many pennies as they can in one minute. Each child gets to keep the pennies he collects (at the end of the game, have each child place her pennies in her personalized favor bag). For an indoor hunt, have the children find the pennies you have hidden and carry them in the strainers or bags.

3. Johnny's Sing-Along • (Use your child's name) If you are lucky enough to have found a pianist or guitarist, have him play the songs while the children sing along. Hand out those song sheets you xeroxed. You can also play records and have the kids sing along.

4. Bronco Darts • Put up the Velcro dart board. Give each child three chances to hit the bull's-eye. You can also divide the group into teams.

5. Wild West Scavenger Hunt • This could take between 30 minutes and an hour. If you have planned the Scavenger Hunt to be in your backyard, you can put your child in charge of the hunt.

If you feel comfortable letting the children loose in your neighborhood or apartment building, go ahead, but be sure to set borders and limits. Give each of them a clearly marked map so the kids know where to go. Have adult supervision (at least one adult per team is a good idea). You have already marked the places the teams can go. Be sure you reminded your neighbors that the teams are coming!

* Carol Schneider xeroxed a map of her town (White Plains, New York), circled the area around her house and sent it as the invitation to her son's Scavenger Hunt.

Divide the children into teams. Set a time limit for the hunt. Emphasize that everyone must be back by then. Give each team its list and explain the rules (stick to the maps, one point for each find unless otherwise marked, gather the items in the shopping bags) and go to it! The winning team will have gathered the most items.

Here is a suggested list. Add or subtract, or make up your own. Find the following:

a cowboy hat (not your own)
a blue bandanna
a macaroni noodle
a used stamp
a page of homework with no mistakes
a white hair
a 1984 penny
a cardboard paper towel roll
a water pistol
a bug (1 point dead, 2 points alive)
dust
a Cheerio
a battery
a boot (not your own); 2 points if it's a cowboy boot
a key
a piece of rope
an orange peel
a doctor's signature
a piece of Christmas wrapping paper
a baseball trading card
a picture of a cowboy
a small bag of Trail Mix
Someone named Mary or Gary (5 points)
a Polaroid picture
a feather
a rhinestone

TIP

Use toys from your child's toy box to decorate the party room. Dump trucks are wonderful receptacles for candy, flowers, favors, etc. Dolls, stuffed animals and plastic toys create instant atmosphere.

When all the children have returned, total the points of the things they have collected. Have prizes ready for the winning team. The kids should be very excited—and a little tired. Now is a good time to gather them together for their picnic.

6. WESTERN ROUND-UP PICNIC

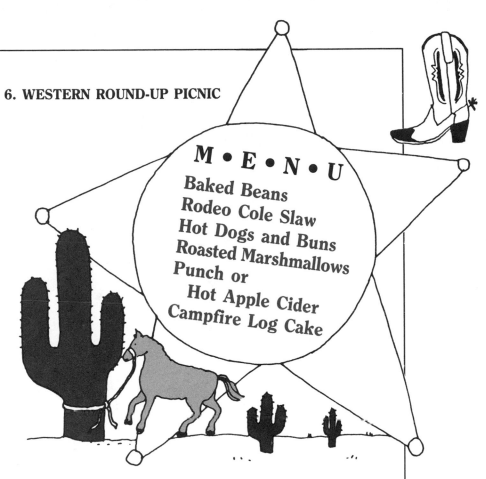

M • E • N • U

Baked Beans
Rodeo Cole Slaw
Hot Dogs and Buns
Roasted Marshmallows
Punch or
Hot Apple Cider
Campfire Log Cake

Serve the picnic in metal pie tins.

See the recipes on page 237.

FAVORS

Suggested favors for this party are red bandannas, sheriff's badges or any cowboy-related items: hats, collar studs, books on knot tying, small-scale horses, cowboys, etc.

✳ Meredith's Aunt Inadoll (that is her real name!) gave a Western party for her kids and served a drink called the "Hailstorm" (punch with lots of ice) in small Mason jars (the kind used for canning). She told the kids why it had that name: It seems that back in the "olden" days, the cowboys rushed out after a hailstorm to collect the ice. It was the only time, except in winter, when they had ice for their drinks!

PARTIES
AWAY FROM
HOME

At one time or another, you will want or need to have your child's party away from home, because your house is being painted, your driveway is being resurfaced, your home has become a temporary hotel for out-of-town relatives, or your child just has to have his party at the zoo this year. This is the time to look to your local resources for choices for such a party—and there may be more available than you might have thought. Discuss the options with your child and make a list of the possibilities. Once you have made your choice, you can still follow our philosophical guidelines about party giving and our many suggestions for unusual invitations and unique party favors. At some places you will even be able to play some of our games. Put that together with the tools you will need to plan this party and the result will be a smooth and happy event.

THE TOOLS

Check It Out

This may seem obvious, but you need to take the time to find out everything you can about the place you have chosen. Here are some questions to ask:

- Has it been the scene for children's parties before?
- Will they provide you with names of people who have given parties there?
- What is the cost per child? Are there any additional charges (room charge, service charge, extra cost for favors, decorations, food, etc.)? Do they require a deposit or the entire amount up front?
- How many people will they provide to help you?
- Do they provide the full entertainment?
- Will other parties be held at the same time?
- Will they provide the birthday cake or do you bring it?
- Do they send out invitations or can you choose and send your own?
- Do they provide picture-taking and/or is that included in the price?
- Can you see a party in progress?

Make Arrangements in Advance

If you know that your child will be having a party away from home, call your choice (or choices) ahead of time. We know many parents who called various places and found that no space was available for their party. One of our friends called the Bronx Zoo in New York to schedule a party a month in advance, only to find out that it was booked for an entire year. Popular places are guaranteed to be booked in advance, so leave yourself enough time to schedule a party to minimize your child's disappointment.

Make the Decisions and Plans with Your Child

As in all our parties, make the decisions with your child. Often, when you plan an event in a place that is used to giving children's parties, the professionals are also used to making the decisions for you. Take the initiative and make the decisions with them and with your child. Include her in the initial visit and the discussions of plans for the party. Let her take part in making choices so she feels as if she is an important part of the process.

Call Others Who Have Been There

A personal talk with another parent who has actually given a party at your chosen location will not only make you feel better but will probably also give you valuable insights and advice. This is the only way you will find out if the entertainment lived up to its billing, if the people who were there to help did indeed help and not hinder, if the food was warm or cold, and if the favors were what you were promised. Someone else's experience will give you the hints you will need to be prepared for this party.

Try to Be Original

One of the drawbacks of giving a party at a public place is that it will not be as original as one you give at home. Such a party at a museum, zoo, or gymnastics studio will be given for many other children, so chances are your child will have already been to a party at the place you chose. What, then, will make this party memorable for your child? What will make it seem that it was given just for him? The answer is found in taking the time to make this predictable occasion less so. You can begin by sending your own invitations, making them as original as the ones we have designed for our parties. If you like, you can bring your own decorations and party favors. If the situation and location warrant it, you can ask that one of your child's favorite games be included. You can make individual photo albums with pictures of the party and keep one for your child and send the others to the guests.

Take Along an Emergency Bag

We call this the "Just in Case" bag. In it are the following items: Band-Aids, LifeSaver candies or small bags of raisins (for the grouchy/hungry child), your doctor's telephone number, individual packets of Wash'n Dris, tissues and change for telephone calls. If the trip to your party location takes more than half an hour, you would be wise to take some paper and pencils (or those ready-to-play "car" games/puzzles you can buy at any toy store) and keep the children smiling rather than restless and impatient. Singing songs is another lifesaver activity; you need no props, just popular suggestions and a loud voice.

PLACES TO PARTY

Here are some suggestions that might be appropriate for giving children's parties. At some, this will be a common event; at others, you may have to use your imagination to help create a wonderful party for your child. As always, keep in mind your child's interests, and don't be put off by an unusual request. If your child loves airports and airplanes, an organized visit to the airport with lunch at a cafe overlooking the landings and takeoffs may be just the perfect solution. The TWA lunch room at the airport may not be the place for many birthday parties, but you can arrange a simple lunch there, and your future pilot will love it. And, by the way, there are small, local airports whose managers love to give tours of the facilities, especially to children.

Museums

Museums offer countless opportunities for arranging interesting and amusing parties. Many cities have a Museum of Natural History, with both permanent exhibitions and traveling shows that fascinate and intrigue children. The *Museum of Science and Industry* in Los Angeles has many hands-on exhibits that children love. The *Museum of Natural History* in San Diego had a superb Dinosaur Exhibit that traveled throughout the country, and the museum arranged birthday parties for both the little and big creatures. The *Museum of Natural History* in New York not only offers space for parties but has a party planner who will organize a group of at least ten (but no more than twenty) five- to ten-year-olds. The themes they offer vary from dinosaurs to an encounter at the Planetarium, and the activities include making fossils. Any planetariums, botanical gardens or visiting navy ships are also naturals for children's parties.

Children's museums everywhere are intrinsic party places. The *Los Angeles Children's Museum* offers parties at the museum. It once even arranged for an all-night party where the children got to see how the city lives at night by visiting a newspaper plant, all-night grocery center, diner, factory and police station (this museum also arranges for staff members to bring games to your home). The *Boston Science Museum* offers not only daytime parties but "camp-in" slumber parties as well (the children get to stay overnight at the museum).

Art museums are also local treasures for children who are art lovers. You can combine a visit to the museum and lunch, and arrange for a hands-on activity for the children to make their own art. If your local art museum does not have such facilities, you can ask an artist or art student to take the children on a tour of the museum and then have the children eat lunch at a nearby restaurant.

Factories

If your child's interests happen to coincide with what this factory produces, you've got it made! Auto plants, newspaper plants, jewelry manufacturers, assembly plants, cookie and milk factories, and so on can schedule tours if you give them enough time. A visit to any of these places, plus a lunch or picnic, makes for a terrific party.

Zoos, Aquariums and the Like. . .

For those animal lovers, the zoo is a fantasy come true. Just remember to call weeks (if not months) ahead of time just to be sure you won't have a scheduling problem. Many cities have aquariums or Sea Worlds. If your child is fascinated by marine life, a party given at one of these havens will not be forgotten.

Pottery Studios

For children who like to work with clay, a trip to a pottery workshop is the answer. There the children can make their own creations and see what a professional does. You can then have the children's projects fired in the kiln and deliver them to the kids at a later time.

If your child loves jewelry making, sewing or any other craft activities, find a shop or studio that may be amenable to letting a bunch of children learn how and what they create.

Gymnastics Studios

The Olympics certainly brought the world of gymnastics home to the children of the world, and they haven't stopped doing headstands since. For the gymnastics fanatic, there are teaching gyms everywhere, and many of them specialize in children's activities. Many cities have gymnastics centers for very young children, and giving parties at such places has become quite popular. Since there is a good chance that your child has been to at least one party at your local gym, try to individualize his party according to our suggestions.

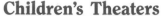

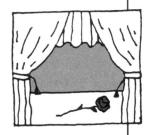

Children's Theaters

These are obvious centers for parties, but again, chances are great that your child will visit such a theater more than once in his birthday party–going life. It's not so bad if the theater changes its program every so often, but even so, you may want to make a point of bringing your own favors and sending a truly creative invitation to make your child's party stand out from the others. If your local children's theater schedules several parties at the same time, try giving your party a theme and having the children come in costume.

Some children love ballet or orchestra performances. If your child is so inclined, and if she is ten or older (their attention span is longer), make arrangements to go to such a performance. Ticket prices are reduced for group sales.

Service-Government Centers

This is a varied group. For the young would-be police officer or fire fighter, you can take the children on a tour of the local police station or firehouse, providing you have made the proper arrangements. Why not have the children come dressed in costume, and give them hats as favors?

Sports Events

For the brave parent of a sports zealot (and one who can call in his chips with several close friends), we suggest a trip to a college or professional baseball, football, soccer or basketball game. This kind of party can be rowdy, hectic and expensive, but it can also be a souvenir of a birthday!

For a participatory sports party, you can give our Baseball party at the park, substituting a baseball game for the Baseball Trivia; an ice-skating party at your local rink; a swimming, soccer or basketball party at the high school or Y (some Y's will help you organize such a party); bowling at an alley; and any other sports that your child loves and you believe to be appropriate for his age.

Take a Real Trip

For those children who either don't travel often or who adore traveling, taking a small trip is fun. You don't even have to have a destination. Taking a bus or train ride to a certain stop and back again is a lot of fun. You can end up having lunch at a cafeteria or a picnic in a local park.

PARTY
MENUS
AND
RECIPES

ARTIST MENU

PAINTER'S PASTA SALAD

Serves about 8 children

- 4 cups tortellini, cooked
- 3 tablespoons vinaigrette dressing
- 3 cups sweet peas
- 2 cups tomatoes, chopped
- 2 teaspoons parsley, chopped
- 1 red pepper, chopped
- 1 cup cucumber, peeled and chopped

Mix all the ingredients together in a bowl and refrigerate.

PICASSO CAKE

- 1¾ cups sifted flour
- 1 cup sugar
- ½ cup butter or margarine, softened
- 2 eggs
- ½ cup milk or cream
- ½ teaspoon salt
- 1¾ teaspoons baking powder
- 1 teaspoon vanilla extract
- 1 teaspoon lemon juice

Preheat the oven to 350 degrees.

Sift together the flour and sugar. Add the other ingredients. Blend in a food processor with the steel blade until smooth.

Grease a sheet cake pan. Pour in the cake batter. Bake for 30 minutes and test for doneness (a knife inserted in the center should come out clean). Let cool, then frost.

SNOW-WHITE JELLY BEAN FROSTING

- 2 cups powdered sugar
- ½ cup sour cream
- 1 teaspoon vanilla extract
- 2 tablespoons butter or margarine, softened
- ½ teaspoon water, if needed
- 3 cups assorted jelly beans

In an electric mixer, blend together all the ingredients except the jelly beans and spread on the cake. Now cover the top of the cake with the jelly beans. If this is a birthday party, stick in the candles and a "Happy Birthday" sign.

BACK TO SCHOOL (OR SCHOOL IS OUT) MENU

CHOCOLATE MINT COOKIES

Makes 28 cookies

- 1 8-ounce package chocolate chips
- 1 cup flour
- ½ teaspoon baking soda
- ½ cup butter or margarine
- ¼ teaspoon vanilla extract
- ½ cup sugar
- 1 egg
- 1 teaspoon mint extract
- 2 tablespoons water

Preheat the oven to 350 degrees.

Melt ½ cup of the chocolate chips in a glass pot or double boiler. Let cool.

Sift together the flour and baking soda. In your food processor using the steel blade, blend the butter, vanilla, sugar and egg until the mixture is creamy. Add the melted

Jill Weber, our designer and illustrator, makes birthday cakes for her son, Remy. She bakes a sheet cake and freezes it. When it is fully frozen, she cuts it into the shape she needs (she has done a bicycle, a cactus, a dinosaur, and an artist's palette). To further prevent crumbling, when you've cut out your shape and before you are ready to frost, brush the cut edges with apricot preserves to seal the cake. Wait for the jam to set and then frost.

chocolate and mint extract, then the water. Keep blending while you add the flour mixture.

Now take the mixture out of the processor and place in a bowl. Add the rest of the chocolate chips and mix carefully with a wooden spoon. You now have chocolate chip mint cookie dough.

Grease two cookie sheets. Drop the cookie dough, 1 teaspoon at a time, 2 to 3 inches apart, on the cookie sheets. Bake for 10 to 12 minutes. Let the cookies cool.

Refrigerate and serve them tomorrow.

BACKWARDS MENU

UGLY CHOCOLATE BIRTHDAY CAKE

Beth Gibbons is the former owner of Tree Top Toys in Washington, D.C. This is her favorite birthday cake recipe.

    2 ounces unsweetened
        chocolate
    1 cup boiling water
    2 cups sugar
    ½ cup butter
    1 teaspoon baking soda
    2 eggs
    2 cups flour
pinch of salt
    ½ cup buttermilk
    1 tablespoon vanilla extract

Preheat the oven to 325 degrees.

Grease and flour two 8-inch cake pans. Melt the chocolate in a double boiler. Add ½ cup boiling water and mix well. Remove from the heat.

Cream the sugar and butter in a food processor or blender.

In a small pan, combine ½ cup boiling water and the baking soda and bring to a boil. Add to the chocolate. Return to the heat and boil for 30 seconds. Cool slightly.

Add the eggs to the butter mixture, beating very well. Mix in the flour and salt, alternating with the buttermilk. Now add the chocolate and vanilla.

Pour into the two cake pans and bake for 30 minutes. When cool, frost.

UGLY FUDGE ICING

    2 cups sugar
    ¼ cup white corn syrup
    2 ounces unsweetened
        chocolate
    ½ cup milk
    ½ cup butter
    1 teaspoon vanilla extract

In a heavy saucepan, mix all the ingredients but the vanilla. Stir until melted and then bring to a boil. Keep stirring for 1 minute. Add the vanilla.

Remove from the heat and beat with an electric mixer until the frosting is lukewarm. Put the pan in ice water and beat again to speed up the cooling process until the frosting is spreadable.

Place both cakes on a cutting board. Ice the top of one. Now place the other cake on the frosted one and frost again. If this is a birthday, you can use candles that won't blow out.

You can substitute 1 tablespoon of orange peel if your child doesn't like mint.

Beth's message: "This cake almost always falls on one side or the other and never looks perfect. It is delicious—a family tradition in our home that always brings smiles to our faces. The frosting is old-fashioned fudge."

BACKYARD BEACH MENU

TYLER'S LITTLE DRUMMERS

Serves 12–16 children

- ½ cup brown sugar
- ½ cup soy sauce (light or mild)
- 2 tablespoons sweet Mirin rice wine (once the chicken is cooked the wine evaporates)
- pinch of ground ginger
- 1 scallion, chopped
- 24 chicken drummettes

Mix all the ingredients except the chicken in a bowl. Pour into one or two glass baking dishes. Add the chicken and marinate for at least 1 hour, turning the chicken from time to time.

Preheat the oven to 350 degrees. Drain the drummettes and reserve the marinade. Bake the chicken for about 30 minutes, basting occasionally with the marinade. Refrigerate and serve cold.

You can keep the drummettes and the marinade in the refrigerator for three days, so try to make them ahead of time. They taste better, and it will mean less work for you the day before the party.

CARROT STICKS

Peel and cut raw carrots into sticks. You can substitute celery, peeled cucumber and zucchini for carrots, if you like.

THUMB PRINT COOKIES

Makes 30 cookies

- 2 sticks (1 cup) butter
- ½ cup sugar
- 2 egg yolks
- 1 teaspoon almond or vanilla extract
- 2 cups flour
- strawberry or any other kind of jelly

Preheat the oven to 350 degrees.

Mix together all the ingredients except the jelly. Roll out ½ inch thick. Now cut into 1-inch squares. Have the birthday child press his thumb on each square and fill that with his favorite jelly.

Bake the cookies for about 12 minutes. Let cool.

SWIMMING POOL BIRTHDAY CAKE

- 1 cup sugar
- ½ cup oil
- 2 eggs
- ½ cup milk
- 1¾ cups sifted flour
- 1 teaspoon milk
- 2 teaspoons baking powder
- 1 teaspoon vanilla extract

Preheat the oven to 350 degrees.

In a food processor with the steel blade (or with an electric mixer), mix the sugar and oil. Add the other ingredients and mix again.

Grease a 9- by 13-inch sheet baking pan. Pour in the batter and bake for 30 minutes. Test for doneness. Let cool, then frost.

TIP

While the children are playing outside, have your helpers set aside an area that is not wet for lunch. This can be on a picnic table, if you have one, or on a picnic blanket. Place the lunch in each pail. You can serve the drinks in paper cups. Be sure to place two large paper napkins in each lunch pail. They'll need it!

TIP

If this is not a birthday party, there is no need for the cake. The kids will have had enough to eat by then. Give them the cookies, and add ice cream or ice cream pops, if you like.

FROSTING

- 2 cups whipped cream cheese
- 1 cup powdered sugar
- 12 drops blue food dye
- 1 graham cracker

Beat together the cream cheese and sugar. Add the blue drops, making it as blue as you like (this is the water in the pool).

To decorate: Frost the cake with the blue frosting on top, leaving the sides plain. (You can also make half the frosting white and the other half blue. There will be enough for both, and that way you can frost the top blue and the sides white.) Decorate with a graham cracker diving board, a miniature ladder (sold wherever you buy doll house miniatures), tiny rubber ducks, miniature floating rafts, etc. (You can use LifeSaver candies as little floaties.)

BALLET MENU

AUNT CORA'S CAKE

- 3 cups sifted flour
- 3 teaspoons baking powder
- ½ teaspoon salt
- 1½ sticks (¾ cup) unsalted butter, softened
- 2 cups sugar
- 1 teaspoon vanilla extract
- 1 teaspoon almond extract
- 1 cup milk
- 6 egg whites

Preheat the oven to 375 degrees. Grease and lightly flour two 9-inch cake pans. Set aside.

Sift the flour, baking powder and salt together. Set aside.

Cream the butter and 1½ cups of the sugar together until fluffy. Mix in the vanilla and almond extracts. Add the flour mixture in four parts, alternating with the milk. Whisk the egg whites and, when foamy, start adding the remaining ½ cup sugar, continuing to beat until eggs stand in stiff peaks. Fold into the batter with an over and under motion. Pour into the two pans and bake for 35 minutes, or until a cake tester comes out clean.

Allow the cake to cool slightly and loosen the edges before removing from the pans. Ice with the following:

ICING

- 1 cup boiling water
- 2¼ cups sugar
- 1 tablespoon white corn syrup
- 3 egg whites
- 1 teaspoon vanilla extract

Combine the water, 2 cups of the sugar and the corn syrup and cook at a rolling boil until the mixture reaches 238 degrees on a candy thermometer (it spins a thread).

Meanwhile, whisk the egg whites; when they are foamy, start adding the remaining ¼ cup sugar. Continue whisking until the whites stand in peaks.

When the syrup reaches the correct temperature, pour into the

This recipe, given to us by Lee Bailey, is a special treat. His aunt, Cora Bailey, always served this cake for birthdays, decorated with candy canes and crushed peppermint sprinkled on top. The recipe calls for white boiled icing, but the icing can be dyed pink and peppermint extract can be substituted for the vanilla. In between the peppermint sticks, perch one or two of your plastic ballerinas and a swan, if you like, add a birthday sign and candles, and you're ready to celebrate!

beaten egg whites in a thin, steady stream, beating all the while. Use to fill between the layers of the cake and ice the top and sides. Hold layers together with tooth-picks, if necessary.

Now decorate with the peppermint sticks, crushed peppermint, ballerinas and/or swans.

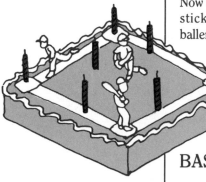

BASEBALL MENU

BASEBALL DIAMOND CAKE

1¾ cups sifted flour
1 cup sugar
½ cup butter or margarine, softened
2 eggs
½ cup milk or cream
½ teaspoon salt
1¾ teaspoons baking powder
1 teaspoon vanilla extract
1 teaspoon lemon juice

Preheat the oven to 350 degrees.

Sift the flour and sugar. Add all the other ingredients. Blend in a food processor with the steel blade until smooth.

Grease a sheet cake pan. Pour in the cake batter. Bake for 30 minutes and test for doneness (a knife inserted in the center should come out clean). Let cool, then frost.

FROSTING

2 cups powdered sugar
½ cup sour cream
1 teaspoon vanilla extract
2 tablespoons butter or margarine, softened
colored frostings in tubes (the same colors you used for your teams in the games)
shredded coconut
green food coloring
graham crackers, optional

In your food processor or with an electric mixer, blend the sugar, sour cream, vanilla and butter. Spread on the cake.

To decorate (see illustration): Tint the coconut with the food color-ing and spread it over the cake. Place the cake facing you as if it were a diamond. Make four squares ("bases") at the corners. You can draw them with one color of frosting or use graham crackers. Place two or three baseballs in the middle. Place the baseball figures at the different bases. Use the other frosting color to write a message, and arrange your candles strategically.

BIKE-A-THON MENU

RACER'S FRIED CHICKEN
Serves 10 children

3 whole chickens, fresh, cut into pieces
salt, to taste
2 cups flour
1–2 cups safflower oil

220

The secret is using fresh chicken. The day before the party, buy and make the chicken.

Wash and dry the chicken. Put a piece of wax paper on the counter and spread the chicken on it. Sprinkle with salt on all sides. Put the flour in a paper bag. Drop 2 to 3 chicken pieces at a time into the bag and shake well, until the pieces are completely covered. You may need to add more flour.

Place the chicken on a platter and refrigerate for 1 hour to let the flour adhere to the chicken.

Heat the oil in a deep fryer to very hot. (To test, put water drops into the oil. If it sizzles, it is ready.) Fry 3 to 4 pieces at a time, uncovered, until the chicken is brown on all sides. (One breast will take about 15 minutes.) When each piece is done, remove and drain on paper towels. Store, wrapped, in the refrigerator and serve the next day.

SPOKE CAKE

You will be making two cakes. This recipe is for one cake.

1¾ cups flour
  3 teaspoons baking powder
½ cup butter or margarine
1½ cups sugar
  3 eggs
⅔ cup milk
  1 tablespoon vanilla extract
½ teaspoon anise (optional—
    use only if your child
    loves the taste of licorice)

Preheat the oven to 375 degrees.

Sift together 1¾ cups flour and the baking powder. Then sift them again.

In a food processor, blend the butter. Gradually, a tablespoon at a time, add the sugar. When well blended, add the eggs while still mixing (wipe off the sides of the bowl every now and then).

Alternately add the flour and milk to the butter mixture, 1 tablespoon at a time. Add the vanilla and, if desired, anise, and mix again for about 15 seconds.

Grease and flour one 8- or 9-inch round cake pan. Place in the center rack of the oven and bake for 35 minutes. Test for doneness. Remove from the oven and turn it over onto a cutting board or platter. Let it cool for *1 hour* before frosting.

FROSTING

? cups powdered sugar
3 tablespoons butter or
    margarine
pinch of salt
1 tablespoon vanilla extract
2 tablespoons heavy cream
2 packages black licorice strips
2 licorice discs

Sift the sugar. In a food processor with the steel blade, blend the butter until smooth. Gradually add the sugar until creamy. Then add the salt and vanilla. Don't worry if the consistency is off; you can fix it by adding the cream.

Don't use cold ingredients—the cake will bake better if the ingredients are at room temperature.

Annie's mother-in-law, Sylvia Gilbar, loves coconut and has been known to tint it in a variety of colors. Here's how she does it.

  To color coconut: Place 2 cups of coconut in a glass bowl. Add 3 to 4 drops of food coloring and mix with a plastic spoon until you get a shade you like. It's better to start with just a few drops of coloring since you can always add more to get the color you prefer.

This frosting is caramel colored. If you want a real white frosting, use the one on page 231 from the Drum Cake.

Here's an old-fashioned hint from Meredith's mom: To get a shiny look to your frosting, use a plastic spatula and dip it in hot water every now and then while you are spreading the icing on the cake.

Before dinner is served, have the girls bake the cake. You can make the tacos while the girls are learning cheerleading or wait and have them make the tacos with you. Serve ice cream and toppings after they eat the tacos; by then the cake should be ready.

If this is a birthday party, have several tubes of ready-made frosting at hand and let the children write the birthday message. Then add the candles and you have a birthday cake the girls made themselves.

When the cakes are cool, frost them on all sides.

Now take the licorice strips and make a wheel rim and spokes on the cakes. Use a licorice disc for the center.

CHEERLEADING MENU

TACOS

Serves 12 children (2 tacos each)

**6 pounds lean ground beef
pinch of garlic powder, optional
24 slices tomatoes
2 cups shredded Cheddar
cheese
shredded lettuce (2 medium
heads iceberg lettuce)
24 taco shells**

In a large cast-iron saucepan, brown the beef. Don't add any fat—there's enough there to prevent the meat from burning. If your child likes garlic, you can add a bit of garlic powder. When done, stuff each taco with about 3 to 4 tablespoons of meat, 1 slice of tomato, 2 tablespoons of Cheddar cheese, and some shredded lettuce.

ICE CREAM SUNDAES

**any ice cream flavors you like
toppings: chocolate syrup,
strawberries, blueberries,
marshmallows, M&Ms,
colored sprinkles, chopped
nuts, sliced bananas**

The children can help themselves to these sundaes. Just put everything out on a table that has been covered with a disposable plastic tablecloth. Place each of the toppings in glass bowls (you will probably need about 3 cups of each topping) with spoons in them. Have a lot of napkins handy.

WACKY CAKE

Let the children make this cake together. It is easy and fun—made right in an 8- by 8-inch baking pan.

**1½ cups flour
1 cup sugar
3 tablespoons cocoa
1 teaspoon baking soda
½ teaspoon salt
1 tablespoon vinegar
1 teaspoon vanilla extract
6 tablespoons salad oil
1 cup water
3 tablespoons powdered
sugar**

Preheat the oven to 350 degrees.

In the baking pan, sift the flour, sugar, cocoa, baking soda and salt. Make three holes in the mixture (you can press in a soup ladle and remove). Pour the vinegar in one hole, the vanilla in another and the salad oil in the third. Now pour the water over the entire mixture and mix with a fork just until all the lumps are out.

Bake for 25 to 30 minutes.

To decorate: This trick will amaze the children:

Hold a paper doily over the cake and sift the powdered sugar on it. The sugar that goes through the holes will form a pretty pattern on the cake.

GHOST MENU

GHOST SANDWICHES

Make these in the morning. Take one slice of bread for each child (and make a few extras). Lightly toast and cool. Cut out each slice with a gingerman cookie cutter. Now spread with cream cheese, make two eyes with raisins and put one on each plate.

SLIME JELL-O

Make lime Jell-O according to the package instructions. Make it in large glass baking dishes. When serving, don't cut it neatly. Slop it on each plate with a large serving spoon. And make a point of calling it "slime" when serving it to the children. They'll love it when you announce, "Anyone for more slime?"

SPOOK CAKE

2½   cups all-purpose flour
1½   cups sugar
** 1   teaspoon salt**
** 3   teaspoons baking powder**
1¼   cups milk
** ⅔   cup safflower oil**
** 2   eggs plus 2 egg yolks**
** 2   teaspoons vanilla extract**

Preheat the oven to 350 degrees.

Grease and flour a 9- by 13-inch baking pan (you can make a thinner cake in an 11- by 15-inch pan) or the gingerbread pan.

In a large bowl, mix together the flour, sugar, salt and baking powder. In a food processor using the steel blade, blend the milk and oil. Add the flour mixture and blend well for about 2 minutes. Now add the eggs and vanilla and blend again until the batter is very smooth (another 2 minutes).

Pour the batter into the baking pan. Bake for 40 to 50 minutes, or until ready when tested. (Insert a knife in the middle; if it comes out clean, the cake is ready.) Let it cool for at least 1 hour before frosting. When cool, cut, with a sharp knife, into the shape of a ghost. Now make the frosting.

SPOOK FROSTING

¾   cup butter, softened
4   cups powdered sugar
⅓   cup heavy cream
1   tablespoon vanilla extract

Place the butter in a food processor with the steel blade.

TIP:

You can easily make this cake into a ghost form by baking it in a gingerbread cake pan and frosting the finished cake with white frosting. (The gingerbread cake pan can be ordered by mail for $6.49 plus shipping and handling from Wilton Enterprises, Inc., 2240 West 75th Street, Woodridge, IL 60517 or by phone, [312] 963-7100. Be sure to include the catalogue stock number, 2105-P-2072, when placing your order.)

TIP

You may want to try the sugar cube trick before the party just to get the hang of it.

TIP

This 4-layer Half Cake should be sliced thinly as it is very high. If you like, you can make two Half Cakes made of 2 layers each and place them at angles to each other on a large platter. If you are having more than eight to ten kids, double the recipe and make four half cakes.

Blend until it is light and smooth. Keep beating while you add the sugar 1 cup at a time. When well blended, add the cream gradually, then the vanilla. Keep blending until the frosting is smooth and easy to spread.

Frost the Spook Cake on all sides. Refrigerate until morning, when the cake will be ready to decorate.

To decorate: Dip 2 sugar cubes into ½ teaspoon of lemon extract each. Place 2 marshmallows on the cake to be eyes, and put one dipped sugar cube on each marshmallow. When everyone has finished his Ghost Sandwiches and Slime Jell-O, place the cake in the center of the table and light the eyes with a match. The ghost will suddenly "spook" everyone. If this is a birthday party, add the candles now (place them strategically around the head of the ghost so they won't interfere with the firing eyes).

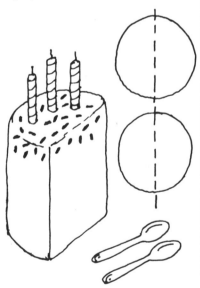

½ BIRTHDAY MENU

The half lunch is a guaranteed hit. You already created the mood by setting the table with halves of everything. Now let's tackle the food:

VIVIAN'S "HALF A ROUND" CAKE

- 1¾ cups sifted flour
- 1¼ cups sugar
- 1 tablespoon baking powder
- 1 teaspoon salt
- ⅓ cup (5⅓ tablespoons) softened butter or margarine
- 1 cup milk
- 1 tablespoon water
- 1 egg
- 1 teaspoon vanilla extract

Preheat the oven to 375 degrees.

Sift the flour again. Then sift the sugar, baking powder and salt and add to the flour. Place in a food processor with the steel blade (or you can use an electric mixer). Add the butter, milk, water, egg and vanilla to the dry ingredients and mix.

Grease two 8-inch round non-stick pans. Pour the batter evenly into both and bake for 25 minutes.

Let cool for 15 minutes. Turn over into 2 platters (if the cake sticks a little, just shake the plate and it will slide out). Let it cool again for another 10 minutes. Meanwhile, make the frosting.

VIV'S LEMON ICING

  2 egg whites, unbeaten
1½ cups sugar
  3 tablespoons water
  ¼ teaspoon cream of tartar
  2 tablespoons lemon juice
  ½ teaspoon grated lemon
     rind
  1 teaspoon vanilla extract
sprinkles

Combine all the ingredients in the top of a double boiler.

Set your timer for 7 minutes. As the water bubbles in the bottom of the double boiler, beat the ingredients in the top with an electric mixer. When done, remove from heat and let cool for about 7 minutes.

Now cut each cake in half. This results in 4 halves. Take one half and frost the top. Top with another half and repeat until the Half Cake is 4 layers high. Now frost the entire cake, including the straight edge. For added color, sprinkle with colored sprinkles. Decorate with the number of candles equal to half your child's age. If it's an odd number, cut a candle in half.

MAD HATTER TEA PARTY MENU

LADYFINGERS WITH PEANUT BUTTER

As easy as it sounds! Take two ladyfingers per person. Place them open on your cutting board and spread with peanut butter. Close each and place on a pretty platter.

CUCUMBER HEARTS

Place slices of white or dark bread, crusts removed, on a cutting board. Spread with a thin layer of margarine. Place sliced cucumbers on each and cover with another slice of bread. Place on a platter and cut out each sandwich with the heart-shaped cookie cutter.

LYNNE'S DOUBLE CHOCOLATE CHIP BROWNIES

Makes 30 brownies

  ¾ cup flour, sifted and
     re-sifted
  ¼ teaspoon baking soda
  ¼ teaspoon salt
  ⅓ cup sweet butter or
     margarine
  ¾ cup sugar
  2 tablespoons water
  2 cups semi-sweet chocolate
     chips
  1 teaspoon vanilla
  2 eggs
  1 cup walnuts or pecans,
     optional (roasted in
     toaster oven)

Preheat the oven to 325 degrees.

Meredith's mom's "Seven Minute Frosting" was a favorite in their house. It takes 7 minutes to cook it, but beware: it may take the kids just about 2 minutes to eat it!

225

For additional baking and cake-decorating ideas, we recommend these books: *Cookies for Kids*, published by Better Homes and Gardens (Meredith Corporation, 1716 Locust St., Des Moines, IA 50336; 1983; ISBN 0-696-00865-3, $5.95); *1987 Wilton Yearbook: Cake Decorating* (Wilton Enterprises, Inc., 2240 West 75th St., Woodridge, IL 60517; 1986; ISBN 0-912696-37-0; $3.99); and *Children's Birthday Cake Book*, published by The Australian Women's Weekly (Australian Consolidated Press, Ltd., 168 Castlereagh St., Sydney, Australia; $9.95).

In a small bowl, combine the flour, baking soda, and salt. Set aside. In a small saucepan, combine the butter, sugar and water. Bring just to a boil. Remove from the heat and add 1 cup chocolate chips and vanilla. Stir well until everything has melted.

Transfer the melted mixture to a large bowl. Add the eggs, one at a time, beating all the time. Now gradually blend in the flour mixture by hand. Add the remaining 1 cup of chips and the nuts, mixing gently (we use a wooden spoon so the chips won't break).

Grease a 9-inch-square glass baking dish. Pour in the brownie mixture and spread so it is even in the dish.

Bake for 30 to 35 minutes. Let cool, and slice into 1½-inch squares.

MAD HATTER ABSOLUTELY SINFUL M&M BIRTHDAY CAKE

- ¾ cup unsweetened cocoa powder
- ¾ cup boiling water
- ½ cup butter or margarine, softened
- 2 cups sugar
- 2 eggs
- 1 teaspoon vanilla extract
- 1 cup buttermilk or plain yogurt
- 1½ teaspoons baking soda
- 2 cups sifted cake flour

Preheat the oven to 350 degrees.

Grease and flour two 8- by 2-inch round cake pans. Line the bottoms with wax paper.

In a small mixing bowl, mix together the cocoa and boiling water. With your electric mixer, blend the butter and sugar until smooth. Now add the eggs, one at a time, and then the vanilla. In a food processor with the steel blade, blend together the buttermilk and baking soda.

With the electric mixer beating, alternately add ½ cup of flour and ½ cup of the buttermilk to the bowl with the butter and sugar. Finally add the cocoa mixture. (You can do all of this in the food processor if you have two bowls.)

Pour the batter into the two cake pans. Bake for about 35 minutes (test for doneness with a knife). When ready, let cool for about 30 minutes before frosting.

CHOCOLATE FROSTING

2 tablespoons butter
4 ounces semisweet
    chocolate
⅓ cup heavy cream
1¼ cups powdered sugar,
    sifted
1½ teaspoons vanilla extract

In a small saucepan, melt the butter and chocolate. Stir constantly until melted and smooth. Add the cream and stir again. Remove from the heat and add the sugar and vanilla. Beat with a whisk until smooth.

Decorating the Cake: Place the cake on a large cake platter. Frost the top only. Place the other layer on top and frost the top of the now 2-layer cake. Take a 4-inch satin ribbon and wrap it around the entire cake (the part that is not frosted). Tie at one end in a large, pretty bow. (To practice making this bow, try wrapping and tying it around a garbage pail.) Completely cover the top of the cake with M&Ms (it will take 2 to 3 cups). Place the cake in the center of the table for the entire party. When you are ready to cut the cake, remove the ribbon.

That's it! You now have a Mad Hatter Absolutely Sinful M&M Birthday Cake!

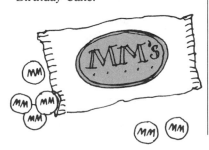

MAGIC MENU

PITA ROLL-UPS WITH SURPRISE FILLINGS

Take pita breads and cut in half. Spread each half with one of the following fillings:

**peanut butter, thin slices of bananas and raisins
creamy tuna salad
any thinly sliced luncheon meat, cheese and garnish**

Roll up each pita half and fasten with a toothpick. Refrigerate.

HIDDEN SECRETS MAGIC CAKE

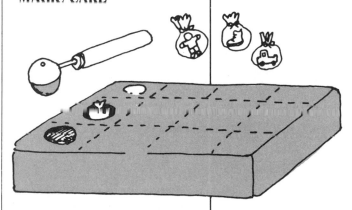

Make the cake recipe for a sheet cake, but don't frost it. Score the cake with a knife to make 2-inch-square servings of cake (do not cut through the cake). When the cake is cool, turn it upside down and scoop out with a melon scoop every 2 inches or so (you are making one scoop in each 2-inch square that you scored).

If you choose to use a canned chocolate icing instead of making your own, you should refrigerate it first so that it will harden and be easier to spread.

Make sure the children don't eat the cake until they find the surprises!

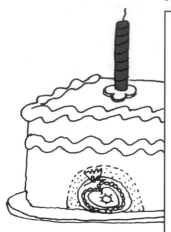

Use uncooked broccoli rather than frozen—it stands up firmer and will be fresh to eat.

Wrap tiny toys or charms in plastic baggies tightly. Insert one into each scoop, until all the scoops are filled (you need one square of cake for each child). Put the cake on a cake platter or cutting board and then turn it over.

Frost the cake, marking the scored sections with a knife or fork pattern. Refrigerate.

When ready to serve, tell the children each piece will have a hidden magic surprise. Cut the pieces where they were scored and serve. Let the children find the surprises with their plastic spoons.

MAKE-UP MENU

ROAST BEEF WRAPPERS

Serves 6 children (2 sticks each)

- 2 **tablespoons Dijon mustard**
- 2 **tablespoons mayonnaise**
- 12 **slices prepared roast beef or smoked turkey**
- 12 **sticks carrots, cucumbers or celery (or all), peeled**

In a small bowl, mix together the mustard and mayonnaise. Spread a little of this mixture on each slice of meat. Wrap a slice around one of the vegetable sticks. Repeat.

When done, wrap each in foil and refrigerate. Serve at room temperature.

VEGETABLE LADIES

sprigs of broccoli
pimento olives
cherry tomatoes
slices of lemon peel

Make each sprig of broccoli, 2 to 3 inches high, into a face. Under the top, place 2 olives for eyes, add the tomatoes for hands and use a slice of lemon peel for the mouth.

Serve with the Roast Beef Wrappers.

ICE CREAM CAKE

- 3 **quarts ice cream (you can use three different flavors your child adores)**
- 1 **package Oreo cookies**

Let the ice cream soften in your sink. Meanwhile, take a springform cake pan and spread the bottom and sides with Oreo cookies. Spread one flavor of ice cream flat on the bottom. Layer with more Oreo cookies. Now spread with the second flavor. Add cookies again, and then another layer of the third flavor of ice cream. Finally cover with the last layer of Oreo cookies. Freeze.

When ready to serve, open the spring pan, place on a platter and serve.

OLYMPICS MENU

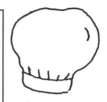

CHAMPION SANDWICHES

**egg or wheat bread, at least
2 slices per person
any filling you like (make it
simple, like peanut butter
and jelly or salami and
cheese)**

Cut the crusts off the bread. Make the sandwich. Now cut it with a large star-shaped cookie cutter (get one that is the size of the slice of bread).

AWARD-WINNING ALL-STRIPE JELL-O

Serves 24–26 children

**5 3-ounce boxes of Jell-O
(different colors)
7 envelopes Knox Gelatin
1 can condensed milk**

Combine each box of Jell-O with one envelope of the gelatin in separate containers. Dissolve each with 1 cup boiling water. (Don't do more than 2 boxes at a time as the gelatin sets very quickly.) Pour the first flavor Jello-O into a 9- by 13-inch glass dish sprayed with Pam for easy removal and refrigerate for 20 minutes.

Dissolve 2 envelopes of the gelatin in ¼ cup cold water. Now add ¾ cup boiling water. Combine the condensed milk and 1 cup boiling water. Now add the dissolved gelatin mixture. Divide this entire mixture into 4 equal parts.

After the first layer of Jell-O has set, carefully pour the first ¼ of the milk mixture on top. This will form a second layer of color. Set in the refrigerator for another 20 minutes. Thereafter, alternate a Jell-O color and milk color in layers, refrigerating for 20 minutes after each layer. End with a Jell-O layer.

Refrigerate until you are ready to serve. You can make this a couple of days before the party.

HERO CUPCAKES

Makes 9 cupcakes

**1 cup butter or margarine,
softened
2 cups sugar
3 eggs
3 cups all-purpose flour,
sifted
½ teaspoon baking soda
½ teaspoon salt
1 cup buttermilk or plain
yogurt
2 tablespoons lemon or
lime juice
2 tablespoons grated lemon
or lime zest**

Preheat the oven to 325 degrees.

Grease a 9-cup muffin pan. If you like, you can use paper liners (they really make the cupcakes prettier and are neater to eat). In a food processor with the steel blade or with your electric mixer, blend together the butter and sugar until soft and smooth. Add the eggs, one at a time.

In another bowl, sift together the flour, baking soda and salt. Mix

You can serve lunch in the middle of the events or after the Medal Awards Ceremony. Serve it on a picnic table, on picnic blankets or any other way you like. Just make it simple! And be sure to have all kinds of drinks available for the children throughout the games. Having paper cups and pitchers of Gatorade, lemonade, punch or water on a table at all times will be great for the children and will save you a lot of running around getting drinks on request.

into the butter mixture, alternating with the buttermilk. Now add the lemon juice and zest.

Pour the cupcake batter into the greased muffin pan, filling each cup ¾ full. Bake in the middle of the oven for 30 minutes (test for doneness with a knife; if it comes out clean, the cupcakes are ready).

Cool for 15 to 30 minutes.

LEMON ICING
2½ cups powdered sugar
½ cup lemon or lime juice
2 teaspoons vanilla extract

In your food processor with the steel blade, mix all the ingredients until smooth.

To frost you can spread with a knife or dip each cupcake upside down into the icing.

Now decorate with the flags and/or candles for a birthday. If you have the time and inclination, write each child's name on a cupcake. But don't feel that you have to—there is enough to do at this party!

ORCHESTRA MENU

Remember, we are keeping it simple. Order pizzas and serve the cake with any drinks your child loves.

DRUM CAKE
2 cups flour
2 cups sugar
1 teaspoon baking soda
1 cup butter or margarine
1 cup water
⅓ cup unsweetened cocoa
2 eggs
½ cup buttermilk or plain yogurt
1½ teaspoons vanilla extract

Preheat the oven to 350 degrees.

Grease and flour two 9-inch round cake pans. In a large mixing bowl, mix the flour, sugar and baking soda.

In a small saucepan, heat the butter, water and cocoa until very hot but not boiling. Add to the flour mixture and mix well in a food processor with the steel blade or with an electric mixer. Now add the eggs, buttermilk and vanilla and beat again. Don't worry if the batter looks thin.

Pour the batter into the two cake pans. Bake for 30 minutes (test for doneness with a knife).

Cool the cakes for about 15 minutes and then remove to cake platters so they are ready for frosting.

When placing the cake on the table, surround it with some of the instruments you made.

WHITE FROSTING

¾ **cup sugar**
½ **teaspoon cream of tartar**
2 **egg whites**
¼ **cup cold water**
2 **teaspoons vanilla extract**

In the top of a double boiler (we prefer the glass kind), simmer the sugar, cream of tartar, egg whites and the water. Beat this mixture with an electric mixer until the frosting looks like well-beaten egg whites (about 5 to 7 minutes). Remove the top part of the double boiler and continue beating until the frosting stands in peaks. Now beat in the vanilla.

Frost the top of one layer of the cake quite thinly. Now top the cake with the other cake and frost completely on all sides. Refrigerate, covered, until the morning of the party. Then decorate: Take regular lollipops and arrange in triangles on the side of the cake (see illustration). These will form the sides of the drum. You can top the cake with two chopsticks in place of drumsticks.

ORIENTAL MENU

Serve the chow mein noodles and snow peas plain, uncooked, in individual Chinese soup bowls (or, for younger children, in Chinese teacups).

SNOW PEAS

Snip off the ends and string. You can serve them fresh, or blanch them and dip immediately in ice water for a crunchy treat.

PINEAPPLE BARBECUED SPARERIBS

Serves about 12 children

10 **pounds spareribs (pork spareribs are leaner and thinner, making them easier for the kids to handle)**
12 **whole black peppers**
6 **whole cloves**
2 **bay leaves**
2 **cloves garlic**
Pineapple Barbecue Sauce (recipe follows)

Place the spareribs in water to cover. Add the seasonings. Bring to a boil, cover, and simmer for 30 minutes. Drain, cover and refrigerate until ready to use.

Cook over a barbecue grill for 30 minutes, turning occasionally. During the last 15 minutes, baste with the Pineapple Barbecue Sauce and cook until the ribs are glazed and tender. Remove and place on a platter.

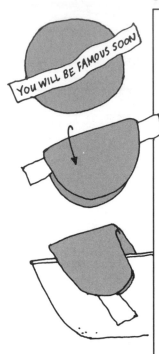

PINEAPPLE BARBECUE SAUCE

- 2 tablespoons brown sugar
- 2 medium onions, finely minced
- ⅔ cup soy sauce
- ¼ cup catsup
- 1 16-ounce can crushed pineapple with syrup
- ⅔ cup dry white wine
- ½ teaspoon ground black pepper
- 1 teaspoon salt

Combine all the ingredients and serve with the ribs.

MADELINE'S FORTUNE COOKIES

Makes 15 cookies

- ½ cup sugar
- 2 egg whites, unbeaten
- pinch of salt
- ¼ cup butter or margarine, melted
- ¼ cup flour
- ¼ teaspoon vanilla extract

Prepare 15 fortunes on 2½- by ½-inch slips of paper. Make them funny and/or sweet: "You are So Smart," "What a Fab Person You Are," "You Will Be Famous Soon!" etc.

Preheat the oven to 350 degrees.

In a mixing bowl, stir the sugar into the egg whites. Add a pinch of salt. When the sugar is fully dissolved, add the butter, flour and vanilla and beat with a mixer until smooth.

Grease a cookie sheet. Drop the batter, one teaspoon at a time, 2 inches apart, on the cookie sheet. Bake for 5 minutes, or until the edges are brown.

Remove the cookies from the oven and put them on a wooden cutting board. Put a fortune across the center of each circle of cookie and fold over to a semicircle. Lay the semicircle on the edge of a mixing bowl and bend it over the outside; hold it there for a few seconds until it holds the shape. Keep working fast until all the cookies are made.

UMBRELLA CUPCAKES

Makes 12 cupcakes

- 1¾ cups sifted flour
- 1 cup sugar
- ½ cup butter or margarine, softened
- 2 eggs
- ½ cup milk
- ½ teaspoon salt
- 1¾ teaspoons baking powder
- 1 teaspoon vanilla extract

Preheat the oven to 375 degrees.

Sift the flour and sugar together. Now sift them again. Add the other ingredients. Blend in a food processor with the steel blade or beat with your electric mixer for 3 minutes.

Grease a 12-cup muffin pan or line with paper cups. Fill each about ⅓ full. Bake for 20 to 25 minutes. Double the recipe if you need more cupcakes.

When cool, decorate with the miniature paper umbrellas.

You have to work fast once you remove the cookies from the oven—you can mold them only while they are hot, and they cool quickly.

232

PIRATE TREASURE HUNT MENU

For many children a lunch with sandwiches and cake is plenty. If, however, you want another dish, we have included the salad.

PIRATE SANDWICHES

These are easy—you had enough work making the cake yesterday! Make one per child and then make half a dozen extras.

bread slices, no crusts
sliced Cheddar cheese
sliced ham

Choose any bread you like. Cut off all the crusts and toast lightly. Place on the counter and cover each with a slice of cheese and of ham (the pre-sliced kind is easier to cut). Cover with another piece of bread and cut with a cookie cutter in the shape of an "X."

CAPTAIN'S SALAD

Serves 8 children

- 2 cups apples, cored, peeled and chopped
- 1½ cups cubed Cheddar cheese
- ½ teaspoon orange rind
- 1 cup fresh orange sections or 2 cups canned mandarin oranges
- ½ cup vinaigrette salad dressing or low-fat mayonnaise
- 1 teaspoon lemon juice

The night before the party, combine all the ingredients in a bowl and chill.

When it's time for lunch, serve small scoops on each child's plate.

CROCODILE BREW

Serves 10–12 children

- 3 cups apricot nectar
- 3 cups pineapple or orange juice
- 4 cups ginger ale or 7-Up
- 2 cups orange or lemon sherbet

In a large bowl, combine the apricot and pineapple juices. Just before serving, add the ginger ale. Pour into glasses and top with a tiny scoop of sherbet.

Try to serve it immediately (before the sherbet melts completely).

TREASURE HUNT CAKE

You need *two* Bundt cakes to make one Treasure Hunt Cake, so make this recipe twice, and then glaze the cakes together as per instructions below.

- 1 tablespoon margarine
- 2½ cups unbleached flour
- 1½ cups sugar
- 3 teaspoons baking powder
- ½ teaspoon salt
- ¾ cup orange juice
- ¾ cup oil
- 2 teaspoons lemon juice
- 4 eggs

Preheat the oven to 325 degrees.

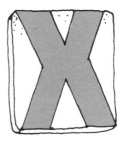

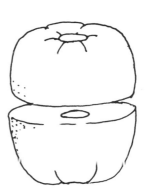

If you don't have an "X"-shaped cookie cutter, cut out the shape on a piece of cardboard and use this as a stencil on the sandwich.

233

TIP

This is a lot of cake for 8 to 12 children (you can feed 24 to 30 children with this cake). But the effect is not the same if you have a small cake. So, even if you have only a few children at this party, make it this size and freeze the rest.

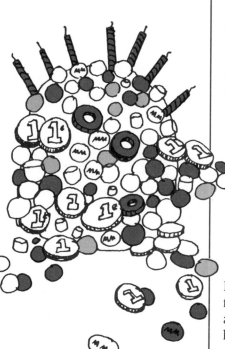

Grease a Bundt cake pan with the margarine. Lightly flour the pan with about 1 tablespoon of the flour.

In a large bowl, using an electric mixer, blend all the ingredients until smooth (about 3 minutes). Pour the batter into the Bundt pan.

Bake for 40 minutes, or until a knife inserted in the middle comes out clean.

If you have another Bundt pan, make the other cake. If not, bake this one and then make it again.

CHOCOLATE FUDGE FROSTING

    4 cups sugar
1½ cups half-and-half
    4 ounces unsweetened
        chocolate bars or 4
        envelopes pre-melted
        unsweetened baking
        chocolate
    4 tablespoons corn syrup
    ¼ teaspoon salt
    4 tablespoons margarine
    2 teaspoons vanilla extract

In a large pot, combine the first five ingredients. Heat, stirring with a wooden spoon, until the chocolate is dissolved. Cover and cook over medium heat for about 2 minutes.

Now uncover the pot and cook for about 20 minutes more. Remove from the heat and add the margarine. Let it cool for about 15 minutes. (Keep watching it so the frosting won't harden.)

Add the vanilla and beat with an electric mixer until the frosting is smooth. If it gets too thick, add some cream.

Now take the two cool Bundt cakes and put them one on top of the other (the flat parts touch). What you'll have are two rounds, one on top of the other, with a hole in the middle. Frost the new cake and let it set in the refrigerator for at least 1 hour.

Now you can decorate it (you can also do that in the morning, if you won't feel too rushed!).

To decorate: Place the frosted chocolate cake on a large platter (and we mean large—use a meat platter or a tray at least 3 feet in length). Buy two large packages of M&Ms; you'll need at least 6 to 8 cups, so get the largest packages you can find. Scoop some of the M&Ms inside the hole in the Bundt cake and distribute the rest on the cake. They should look as if they are falling out of the "treasure hole" in the cake, spilling over to the sides. Now add some of those gold coins you bought for the Treasure Hunt. Buy any other candies you like—marshmallows, hard round candies, the works. Make the cake look as if it is indeed a treasure full of candy jewels.

For the birthday message, buy ready-made frosted letters and spell out your greeting. You can add candles anywhere you like.

SAFARI MENU

ANIMAL SANDWICHES
Figuring one sandwich per child, make as many as you need with any filling your child loves. Then cut the sandwiches with cookie cutters in the shapes of animals.

CELERY STICKS
Cut stalks of celery into 3-inch lengths. Fill the ridge with peanut butter and serve. Two per child should be enough.

SAFARI CHOCOLATE CAKE
- 2 **cups flour**
- 2 **cups sugar**
- ½ **teaspoon salt**
- 1 **teaspoon cinnamon**
- 2 **sticks (1 cup) butter or margarine**
- 3 **tablespoons cocoa powder**
- 1 **cup water**
- ½ **cup buttermilk**
- 2 **eggs**
- 1 **teaspoon vanilla extract**
- 1 **teaspoon baking soda**

Preheat the oven to 350 degrees.

In a large mixing bowl, sift the flour, sugar, salt and cinnamon twice. In a small saucepan, mix together the butter, cocoa and water and bring to a boil. Pour butter mixture over the flour and mix well. In another bowl, mix together the buttermilk, eggs, vanilla and baking soda and then add the chocolate mixture. Mix everything well and pour into a buttered and floured baking dish 11 by 15 inches.

Bake for 20 minutes. When done, let cool for about 10 minutes. Frost the cake while it is still warm.

CHOCOLATE FROSTING
- ½ **cup butter or margarine**
- 1½ **tablespoons cocoa**
- 3 **tablespoons milk**
- 1 **teaspoon vanilla extract**
- 2 **cups powdered sugar**

In a small saucepan, heat the butter, cocoa, milk and vanilla until very hot but not boiling. Then add the powdered sugar and mix well.

Frost the cake. Cover the entire cake with animal cracker cookies (cover the sides and top of the cake, laying the animals flat).

SPACE MENU

ROCKET SANDWICH
Order an extra-long submarine sandwich from your local deli. If your prefer to make your own, get a long French bread and make one sandwich with your child's favorite fixings—cheeses, luncheon meats, tomatoes, pickles, lettuce, etc. When done, put a metal funnel at one end of the rocket.

To make sure your cake unmolds easily, line the bottom of the pan with wax paper *after* you butter it.

235

CRATER CAKE

  1 **package yellow cake mix**
  1 **package lemon pudding**
  2 **teaspoons vanilla extract**
 ¾ **cup oil**
  4 **eggs**
  1 **teaspoon nutmeg**

Preheat the oven to 350 degrees.

Mix all the ingredients in a food processor with the steel blade or with an electric mixer.

Grease and flour a Bundt cake pan. Pour in the batter and bake for 45 minutes. When ready, let it cool for 10 minutes.

Now frost with the chocolate frosting (see the recipe for Treasure Hunt Cake, page 233). Decorate with the astronauts and their ship that you ordered from Wilton.

TAKE A TRIP MENU

AIRPLANE SANDWICHES

Make your child's favorite sandwiches and cut them with a cookie cutter in the shape of an "airplane."

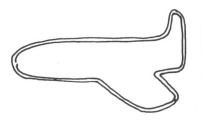

LEMON KISS CUPCAKES

Makes about 25 cupcakes

  2 **cups sifted cake flour**
2⅓ **teaspoons baking powder**
 ¼ **teaspoon salt**
 ½ **cup butter**
  1 **cup sugar**
 ½ **teaspoon lemon juice**
 ½ **teaspoon vanilla extract**
  2 **eggs, separated**
 ⅔ **cup milk**
20 **Hershey Kisses,**
     aluminum removed

Preheat the oven to 375 degrees.

Sift together the flour, baking powder and salt. In a food processor using the steel blade, cream the butter until smooth and gradually add sugar and lemon juice. Cream until fluffy.

Add the vanilla. In another bowl, beat the egg yolks with an electric mixer and add to the butter mixture. Now gradually add the flour, alternating with the milk, and beating until smooth after each addition.

In a second bowl, whip the egg whites until they form peaks. Fold them into the mixture.

Line muffin tins with paper muffin cups. Fill each cup ½ full with batter. Top with a Hershey Kiss. Bake for 25 minutes.

To make the figures stay on the cake, especially the ones you want to appear to be climbing the crater, simply push them right into the cake. They'll look like they're deep into the moon surface and won't fall over.

You can decorate the cupcakes with flags. Put a candle in each cupcake so all the children can blow the candles out at the same time.

WESTERN ROUND-UP MENU

RODEO COLE SLAW

Serves 16 children

- 6 cups shredded cabbage
- ⅔ cup crushed pineapple (drained from a can)
- 1 cup apples, peeled, cored and diced
- ½ cup chopped celery (optional)
- 1 cup mayonnaise
- 2 tablespoons sugar
- 2 tablespoons vinegar
- ½ teaspoon salt

Combine all the ingredients and refrigerate.

CAMPFIRE LOG CAKE

This cake is baked in a 15- by 10-inch jelly roll pan and is rolled into a log shape.

- ½ cup flour
- ½ cup unsweetened cocoa
- 1 teaspoon baking powder
- ¼ teaspoon salt
- 4 eggs, separated
- ¾ cup sugar
- 1 teaspoon vanilla extract
- ¼–½ cup jelly or jam

Preheat the oven to 350 degrees.

Generously butter the bottom of the jelly roll pan. Line with wax paper and grease again.

Combine the flour, cocoa, baking powder and salt and set aside.

Beat the egg whites until foamy. Gradually add half of the sugar to the egg whites, beating constantly until stiff. Set aside.

In a large bowl, beat the egg yolks until thick and lemon-colored. Add the rest of the sugar plus the vanilla; beat until very thick. Add 2 tablespoons water. Now, gradually stir in the flour mixture, folding into the egg yolk mixture after each addition. Gently fold in the beaten egg whites.

Spread the batter in the prepared cake pan. Bake for 18 to 22 minutes, or until the cake springs back when lightly touched. Loosen the edges; immediately turn onto a towel. Starting at the narrow end, roll up the cake in the towel. Cool.

When the cake is cooled, remove the towel. Spread the cake with your child's favorite jelly or jam (or chocolate cream) and roll up again. Frost, run a fork along the frosting to make lines and refrigerate.

FROSTING

Use the Treasure Hunt Cake chocolate frosting on page 234.

ROASTED MARSHMALLOWS

If this is an outdoor picnic, get wooden sticks and roast the marshmallows over a campfire. If it is indoors, you may want to try roasting them in your fireplace. Otherwise, serve them plain.

Serve the meal in metal pie tins.

When you take the cake out of the refrigerator the morning of the party, stick the birthday candles in a row across the log. Push them way down. When you light them, the effect is one of a lighted campfire log. You can also use sparkler candles.

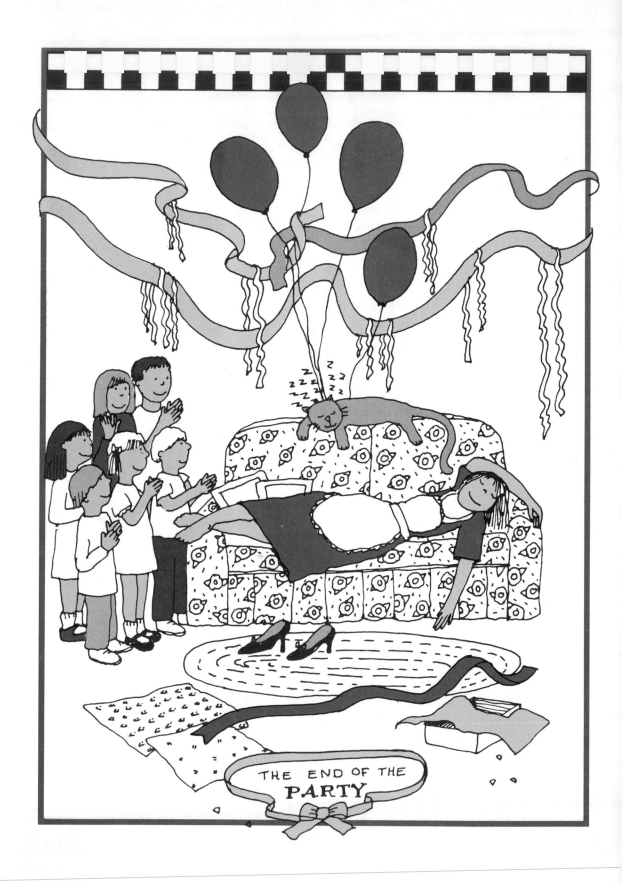

THE END OF THE
PARTY

INDEX

243